Working in Your Major

Working in Your Major

How to Find a Job When You Graduate

Mary E. Ghilani

 PRAEGER

AN IMPRINT OF ABC-CLIO, LLC
Santa Barbara, California • Denver, Colorado • Oxford, England

Copyright 2012 by ABC-CLIO, LLC

Library of Congress Cataloging-in-Publication Data

Ghilani, Mary E., 1958–
   Working in your major : how to find a job when you graduate / Mary E. Ghilani.
      p. cm.
   Includes bibliographical references and index.
   ISBN 978–1–4408–0311–6 (cloth : alk. paper) — ISBN 978–1–4408–2877–5 (pbk. : alk. paper) — ISBN 978–1–4408–0312–3 (ebook) 1. Job hunting. 2. Résumés (Employment) 3. School-to-work transition. 4. Career education. I. Title.
HF5382.7.G45   2012
650.14—dc23   2012014873

ISBN: 978–1–4408–0311–6 (cloth)
       978–1–4408–2877–5 (paper)
EISBN: 978–1–4408–0312–3

16 15 14 13 12   1 2 3 4 5

This book is also available on the World Wide Web as an eBook.
Visit www.abc-clio.com for details.

Praeger
An Imprint of ABC-CLIO, LLC

ABC-CLIO
130 Cremona Drive, P.O. Box 1911
Santa Barbara, California 93116-1911

This book is printed on acid-free paper ∞

Manufactured in the United States of America

Contents

Acknowledgments

Writing a book is never an isolated task—it almost always involves some collaboration with others. Having said that, I would like to thank Jim McAndrew, Associate Professor of Business, Gary Peacock, Inter-Loan Librarian, and David Ehrensperger, Reference Librarian at Luzerne County Community College, for providing me with the initial economic reference material needed to write this book.

Thanks also to Robert Bogdon, Director of Marketing at Luzerne County Community College, for explaining the difference between a blog and an article, and Shirley Yanovitch, Professor of Computer Information Systems at Luzerne County Community College, for the example of a CIS resume that I now use with CIS students.

While I was writing this book, I interviewed Gerry Chrispin, cofounder of CareerXroads, and Chris Russell, CEO/founder of AllCountyJobs.com. Thank you both for your time and expertise. Chris also graciously allowed me to reprint "How to Spot a Good Job Board."

Thanks also to Dr. Thomas J. Denham for permission to reprint "Career Development Myths of College Students."

To write chapter 8, I surveyed professors and department chairs in various disciplines at universities across the country and asked them for their insights regarding the skills graduates needed to be successful in their respective professions. Thank you for your responses.

From Luzerne County Community College:

Dana Charles Clark, EdD RN; Bill Karlotski, Chairperson, Commercial Art; Sheila Malahowski-Davis, HIM Coordinator and Associate

Professor; Andrew Petonak, Instructor, Communications; and Kate Clemente, DEd, RD, LDN.

From the University of Wisconsin–Madison:

Daniel M. Schaefer, Professor and Chair, Department of Animal Sciences; Steven Schroeder, Assistant Dean, Business Career Center, Wisconsin School of Business; Julie Underwood, Dean, School of Education; Dr. David Harwell, Assistant Director, ACS Department of Career Development and Management; Professor Bassam Z. Shakhashiri, William T. Evjue Distinguished Chair for the Wisconsin Idea, and Director, Wisconsin Initiative for Science Literacy; and Rebecca Bertram, RN, BSN, MSN, Clinical Coordinator, School of Nursing.

From the Pennsylvania State University:

Jennifer Hillman, PhD, Professor of Psychology, Penn State Berks Campus; Mitchell Holland, PhD, Director, Forensic Science Program at University Park; Jenifer Smith, Professor of Practice, Forensic Science at University Park; Garry Chick, Recreation, Park, and Tourism Management at University Park; and Charles Ghilani, Professor of Engineering, Penn State Wilkes-Barre Campus.

From Johnson College: Rosemary Cook, CVT, PhD, Sciences Division Chairperson.

Thanks also to Anne Holmes, Professor, Health and Physical Education; Barbara Montante, Associate Professor, Dental Hygiene; and Donna Lepkoski, Professor, Dental Assisting.

A special thank you to my editor, Brian Romer, and the staff at ABC-CLIO.

Lastly, thanks always to my husband, Charles Ghilani, for his encouragement and support.

Introduction

The only way to do great work is to love what you do. If you haven't found it yet, keep looking. Don't settle.

—Steve Jobs

Although the recession officially ended in June 2009, our economy has not rebounded in the way that we expected it would. A 2011 McKinsey report predicts that in the most optimistic scenario, it will take until 2020 before the United States returns to full employment.[1]

What does this mean for the 1,725,000 bachelor's degree and 833,000 associate degree students who are projected to graduate in the class of 2012?[2] It means that you will continue to face stiff competition in the job market—not only from your fellow graduates but from job seekers who are unemployed or seeking to change jobs when the job market improves.

Working in Your Major was written to highlight the important resume, interviewing tips, and job search strategies that you will need to land a job after graduation. Some of the things I hope you will take away from reading this book are:

- Viewing the job search process from the employer's perspective and using that knowledge to better present yourself in a resume or on the interview

- Being able to translate your previous college experience in a way that will show an employer what you can do on the job

- Understanding what employers are looking for in job candidates
- Learning what role your attitude and professionalism plays in the job search
- Learning how to use social media professionally and effectively as a job search tool
- Identifying the best strategies and techniques to successfully find a job in your career field
- Understanding what skills will be required to survive and thrive in the workplace of the future

When I was writing this book, I surveyed professors and department heads of various disciplines at universities and colleges across the country for their perspective on the skills graduates needed to be successful in their profession. Their comments and advice are included in chapter 6, "What Employers Are Looking for in Your Major."

Each career field and each industry has its own rules and methods of finding and hiring applicants. Liberal arts majors often have trouble conceptualizing where jobs might exist because their majors do not directly correspond to a job in the marketplace. That's because they have a wide range of employment options where they can utilize their skills and talents rather than just one industry like accounting or education majors. This concept is discussed further in chapter 4, "Where to Look for Job Openings."

In chapter 5, "The Importance of Social Networking," the concept of traditional networking was expanded to include social media because of the vital role that it now plays in the job search process.

The good news is that you can find a job, regardless of your major, provided you know where to look for openings. Although networking and word-of-mouth referrals are reported as the number one ways to find jobs for job seekers in general, it appears that the best methods for you are right in your school—at career fairs and employer information sessions, where employers are specifically there looking to hire you!

If you're still in college, I encourage you to visit your campus career center. Many students think that the role of career services is to find them a job. But today's career centers have gone beyond simple job placement and can provide you with all of the tools you'll need for managing your career over your lifetime. Even if you've already graduated, most college career centers continue to offer services to alumni, so check it out.

In my experience, the students who are successful in finding a job in their major after graduation, even in a poor economy, are those who tackle the job search process aggressively and utilize a multitude of channels rather than relying on luck or waiting for jobs to find them. To be successful in your job hunt, you need to research your job market, actively search and apply for openings, and demonstrate to an employer that you are a good investment in their future.

The reality of today's workplace is that there is still an abundance of opportunities for skilled workers, despite age or gender. According to the Kinsey report, six sectors have the potential for job growth in this decade: health care, business services (which covers everything from maintenance to business managers to professional services), leisure and hospitality, construction, manufacturing, and retail. These six sectors account for 66 percent of employment today and are predicted to account for 85 percent of the new jobs created through the end of the decade. Education is still the best way to ensure your marketability in an uncertain economic future. The growing trend is that future job openings will require more, not fewer, educated individuals than in the past.

Today, employers are adopting a more balanced view of work and its importance in relation to our personal, spiritual, and physical lives. There are more flexible options available to workers today regarding their daily work schedule and physical work setting, and more opportunities for part-time, temporary, home-based, or freelance work assignments. There is an increased emphasis on social responsibility, in both the way companies treat their employees, and how they manage and treat their environment. The green movement has created lots of exciting, and environmentally responsible, opportunities and will generate more in the years to come. It is a brave new world out there and the future is yours to create!

Again, congratulations on your graduation from college. Approach your future confidently, regard it humbly, and embrace it with joy and anticipation.

ONE

Job Search 101

I'm a great believer in luck, and I find the harder I work, the more I have of it.

—Thomas Jefferson

My first job was working at a pick-your-own strawberry farm. My first introduction to the job search process was overhearing a friend telling another friend that the local strawberry farm was hiring. We now call this process of finding openings through other people "networking." When I asked her what was involved in getting a job there, she said, "All you have to do is fill out an application, then they'll call you in for an interview."

"What happens in the interview?" I asked her.

"Oh, they'll ask you a few questions, like why you want to work there—tell them you really enjoy working with people or something like that," she replied.

Hmmm, not too different from the answers we provide in interviews today.

CAREER MYTHS

There is a lot of advice out there about how to get a job. Some of this advice is helpful, and some of it is just plain wrong. Students hear stories about somebody's Cousin Joe who went to school for eight years, got two master's degrees, and still can't find a job. But what you may not know about Cousin Joe is that he interviews poorly, applies only for jobs that he sees in the Sunday paper, or turned down job offers because of some predetermined (and unrealistic) criteria.

As with everything else in life, myths abound. Dr. Tom J. Denham, career counselor and motivational speaker, and owner of Careers in Transition, wrote a wonderful blog outlining 15 common misconceptions that students have about work[1]:

Career Development Myths of College Students
September 9, 2011 at 5:00 A.M. by Tom Denham

As you begin your career, you will hear conflicting messages and myths about the nature of work. Knowing the truth about these common inaccuracies will improve your chances for career success. Avoid these 15 common misconceptions:

Myth #1: *The most qualified person gets the job.* **Reality:** A strong resume is critical for success so build an outstanding one. Oftentimes, candidates land interviews because they are exceptional networkers. Sometimes offers are made based on the best and most convincing impression, regardless of qualifications. The goal is to sell the best match of your qualifications, "chemistry," and personal attributes for the job.

Myth #2: *My major should always be directly related to my job/career.* **Reality:** The notion that there are no jobs for liberal arts majors or that you have to major in business to land a good job, is false. For example, James Barba, CEO of Albany Medical Center, was a history major at Siena College. Pick a major that you love, and have multiple internships that match your career goals.

Myth #3: *Good grades and a college degree will get me a good job.* **Reality:** A high GPA does not guarantee a job. Today, employers want academic success plus several internships, leadership activities, community service, and technical skills.

Myth #4: *My first job out of college is one that I will be stuck with for a long time.* **Reality:** Most new college graduates are typically in their first job for one to three years. Changing job every three to five years is not job-hopping, and can develop key skills and networking contacts. Avoid very short stints—those under one year. Long-term employment with one firm may signal someone is afraid of change.

Myth #5: *I should know what I want to do before I go to my campus career center.* **Reality:** The career center specializes in students who are undecided, and they will help you get focused and steer you in the right direction. All they ask is that you set up an appointment with one of their career counselors to take self-assessment inventories[,] learn about internships[,] and set goals.

Myth #6: *My family and friends make great career counselors.* **Reality:** It is okay to seek a variety of views, but remember that your family and friends are biased and are not trained career counselors. You will want to have someone listen to you and advise you objectively. Ultimately, your career is your responsibility. Trying to please others, such as your parents or friends, is a mistake that will come back to haunt you in the future. Remember: you, not your parents, must live with your job and career choices.

Myth #7: *I'm going to graduate school; I don't need a resume.* **Reality:** It's a smart idea to begin building your resume now so you can see the gaps in your experience and have time to fill them in before you finish with your education. Graduate school only postpones your job search.

Myth #8: *Interviewing is easy if you know how to talk.* **Reality:** It's a mistake to over-prepare your resume and cover letter, and under-prepare for the interview. In the interview you will need to market and prove yourself as the best candidate for the job. What will you say when an employer asks you to describe your greatest weakness? Set up a mock interview at your career center to work out the kinks in your delivery.

Myth #9: *The only jobs available are in the classifieds.* **Reality:** Most research shows that less than 20% of jobs are ever listed in the classifieds. If someone is looking for a job and the classifieds are their sole source of job leads, their job search will be frustrating because most ads can draw an average of 100 to 300 applicants, and sometimes more. Spend 80% of your job search time networking your brains out!!!

Myth #10: *I sent a resume and a cover letter. If they want me they will contact me.* **Reality:** Given the volume of resumes that most employers receive, a recruiter will spend less than thirty seconds reviewing your resume and cover letter. A passive approach will not work in today's job market; you will need to conduct extensive follow-up and request an interview.

Myth #11: *Money is the most important factor when making a decision about a job offer.* **Reality:** Wrong! Job duties and your new boss are the most important facts. Take into consideration co-workers, typical work week, location, organizational flexibility, work/life balance, tuition reimbursement and vacation time. Compensation is a poor long-term motivator. Job satisfaction should be your top priority.

Myth #12: *The campus career center is the place you go when you are a senior.* **Reality:** Wrong again!! Finding the right career is very time-consuming so don't wait until the last minute. Starting late will only add more stress. Your two main goals are to participate in multiple internships and build your resume. Many seniors remark that they wish they had started this process in their first year in college.

Myth #13: *More education means more marketability.* **Reality:** This is not necessarily true. The key here is to match your professional goals with the right combination of academic credentials and experience. Too often, candidates are well educated, but lack relevant experience. Having a "better" degree does not necessarily mean getting the job you want or getting a job that is meaningful.

Myth #14: *My employer will take care of me.* **Reality:** Perhaps this was true in the 1950s, but in an age of downsizing, the new rule is career self-management. Only you are responsible for advancing your career. Even if you do well for the company, there is no guarantee that the company will guarantee its own future, let alone yours!

Myth #15: *I posted my resume to the Internet, so I should hear about a job offer soon.* **Reality:** The Internet is a part of your overall strategy, but don't spend more than five percent of your job search time on the Internet. Post your resume on three to five of the best job sites and be sure to monitor it as well as checking the job listings on a regular basis. Spend the vast majority of your time networking!

Reprinted with permission from Dr. Thomas J. Denham, http://blog.timesunion.com/careers

ECONOMIC CLIMATE

Many graduates assume that completing their degree is all that is needed to be successful in the professional world. But employment trends are influenced by the current economic climate. The availability of jobs in your geographic area will determine the ease or difficulty of your job search. If you recently earned a highly sought after degree where there are more job openings than applicants, then you probably won't have too much trouble finding a job. In fact, recruiters will probably come to you. This used to be the case in the 1990s for information technology (IT) graduates. And it was the case prior to 2008 for nursing graduates in northeastern Pennsylvania, who were getting $5,000 sign-on bonuses, full tuition reimbursement benefits to earn an advanced degree, and a slew of other perks including full college scholarships for qualified nursing students who promised to work for the sponsoring hospital after graduation. Today, however, it's a different story. Although there are still numerous positions to be had, hospitals are experiencing their own budget problems, and nursing graduates find that they have to compete for coveted positions just like everyone else.

Today there is unlimited access to economic information and numerous ways to access it if you have the time and know-how. Two good sources of labor trend reports can be found at Indeed.com and in the *U.S. Employment Trends Outlook*, published monthly by SimplyHired.com. You can use the data presented in these reports to determine which companies to begin investigating for career opportunities or to determine if the industries you are preparing to enter are experiencing loss or growth.

In February 2012, the U.S. Labor Department reported 3.9 unemployed workers for every job opening (that number was 1.8 in December 2007 and 6.1 in June 2009).[2] The figure shows that unemployed workers outnumber job seekers in every major industry. Keep in mind that these numbers are an *average*; some places are higher, others are lower, and it all depends on the industry.

According to the National Association of Colleges and Employers' (NACE) *2011 Student Survey*, the median time that seniors from the class of 2011 took before landing a job was 7.74 months.[3] Surprisingly, that's up from 6.95 months in 2010.

When a job market exists where there are more jobs than graduates then graduates can literally name their price and their terms. Today it's an employer's market, which means there are many more applicants than there are jobs, and it's probably going to stay that way for a couple of years. College grads find that they're competing against hundreds of equally or better prepared and qualified candidates, many of whom have more experience than they do. Not everyone will be able to work for Fortune 500 companies. In this employment climate, it may be better to work for small to medium-size businesses.

With that said, applicants should begin applying for advertised job openings, making contacts, attending job fairs, and inquiring about future openings as early as possible in their senior year. Having a good resume will help your search immensely, but remember that the resume only gets you in the door. Once you're in the door, how well you conduct yourself in the interview will ultimately determine if you're hired.

Here's some good news if you're an associate degree graduate. Employers that hire associate degree graduates say these students often have more direct work experience than four-year graduates and, as a result, have developed a good work ethic, making them a good choice for entry-level hiring. In addition, they often enter the workforce with a special skill set unique to the positions they seek, so employers need to do less training with these graduates.

About a third of college recruiters note that there is a shortage of new graduates in some specific areas: engineering, computer science, and accounting. If you fall into any of the above categories, then your chances for finding employment are quite good.

DEVELOP A MARKETING STRATEGY

Some people hate it when career experts use the "sales" analogy when talking about finding a job, but the truth of the matter is that trying to convince an employer to hire you is really not that different from trying to sell a car or a house. In both situations you have a product to sell (car or house: your education and skills). To sell these items, there is an established process of highlighting the desired features to the potential buyer (listing/test drive or house tour: resume/interview).

To sell the value of your degree (your value as a potential employee), you're essentially employing the same marketing strategies entrepreneurs and small-business owners use to gain clients or customers. But instead of marketing a product or service, you're promoting yourself as a job candidate.

Any business or marketing major will tell you that in order to promote or sell a product, you need to have an effective marketing campaign. It doesn't have to be clever or multilayered—it just has to be *a plan*. Are you prepared to begin your job search? Do you have a resume, sample cover or e-letter, and three references? How will you look for a job? What method(s) will you use? How will you advertise your availability for positions? Where will you look to find and connect with recruiters? Developing a sound job marketing strategy is crucial when searching for a job. Many students make the mistake of looking at only one source, such as online, or applying to only one or two openings. In a tight job market, a job search strategy has to be multifaceted to be effective.

Here are the components of a sound job marketing plan:

1. Go to your career center and ask them to help you prepare a resume that will professionally highlight your education, work experience, and skills. Even if you already have a resume, go to your career center and have someone proof it for you. Then begin to ask at least three

people, such as professors, clinical or research supervisors, college staff, or work supervisors, if they would be willing to be a reference.

2. Identify your target market. Determine where you want to work (geographic location), and what type of company you want to work for. Will you be looking locally, out of state, or out of the country? Each location will require a slightly different type of approach to find openings and connect with potential employers.

3. Develop a "short" list of target companies. Once you've identified your geographic area, scan the yellow pages in the phone book, search for companies using Yahoo! Directory or Hoovers.com, do a Google search for companies in your industry or career field, or search company directories in LinkedIn. When you have narrowed down your list to a manageable number of potential companies that you would like to work for, check their websites for advertised openings or call/e-mail a human resources (HR) manager and inquire about future openings.

4. Identify methods to find openings. Will you be participating in career fairs, using direct-marketing techniques to target companies, registering with career services, networking at professional organizations and mixers, or applying online? (See chapter 4, "Where to Look for Job Openings," for more information.) Keep a log or spreadsheet to track your progress.

Employers consistently list internships and co-ops as the best source of new full-time employees and look to hire from their internship pool before opening full-time jobs to outside candidates. According to Penn State's Smeal College of Business website, employers convert, on average, 83 percent of their interns into full-time hires.[4] A recent survey of the class of 2011 graduates showed that those who took part in a paid internship were more likely to get a job offer, have a job in hand by the time they graduated, and receive a higher starting salary offer than their peers who undertook an unpaid internship or no internship at all.[5] So what exactly made the difference between a paid versus an unpaid internship? The duties. According to NACE, the paid interns spent more time on "professional" duties—and thus gained more "real" experience—than did unpaid interns, who spent more time on things like clerical activities.

MATCHING YOUR SKILLS TO AN EMPLOYER'S NEEDS

The art of effective job searching is all about finding a match between what the employer needs and what you can offer. The best applicant for the job opening is usually the one whose skills and experience most closely fit the position. In a tight job market where there are more applicants than available positions, applicants will be more successful if they take the "sales approach" and apply for as many openings as they can to increase the odds that at least 10 percent of those applications will result in an interview. Other people have described it as having multiple arrows in your quiver and being able to shoot at many different targets.

Students often ask me if they should bother applying for a job when they do not have *all* of the requirements listed in the job description. I suggest that they apply for the position if they meet the majority of the requirements, especially the critical ones such as a certification or licensure. *Required* generally implies less negotiation, but *preferred* is another story. *Prefer* means that they would *like* to have someone with those qualifications, but it is not absolutely necessary. In other words, you have a better chance of getting the job if you do possess those skills, but you are not automatically out of the running if you don't have those skills.

If a job opening requires five or more years of direct experience, then I probably wouldn't bother applying. However, if the position requires only two to three years of experience, then I would apply and back up the strength of my candidacy by stressing all of the experience I gained during school. Recognize that sometimes employers really don't need *all* of the qualifications that are listed in the position; they are just trying to attract the best candidate they can for the position. The point is, if you don't apply, you will never be considered.

THE APPLICATION PROCESS

Typically, once you apply for a position, whether you've submitted your resume online, to a recruiter, or directly to an employer, it will face some form of keyword screener—in either technology or human form. If your resume makes it through this test, then you may (or may not) receive some form of human confirmation.

After you have submitted your application or resume, the next step in the process is to be contacted by the employer or HR office. They may want to talk to you over the telephone (initial screener) or ask you to come in and fill out more materials, such as a formal application, before scheduling you for an interview.

During the prescreening telephone call or e-mail, the recruiter/company representative will ask some general questions to preliminarily determine if you have the basic qualifications for the position. If there are aspects of the job that will make or break a candidate's qualification, such as willingness to relocate or travel, these will be asked to potentially weed out candidates. Some companies also ask candidates to complete a personality or basic skills test as a part of the applicant screening process.

Those candidates who successfully pass prescreening will be invited in for a formal interview. The interview may be with one person or several. Depending on the position, the candidates may be asked to come in for a second round of interviews, usually with someone higher up the administrative ladder.

Most people believe the purpose of the face-to-face interview is to *identify* the best candidate. But the real purpose, according to an article on CareerCenterToolbox.com, is to *eliminate* candidates. Skip Freeman, author of the article, reproduced a "purpose statement" from an HR manual of a very large Fortune 500 company that read, "The purpose of the face-to-face interview is to *narrow* the initial group of applicants by learning as much about them as you can in a relatively limited time."[6]

This means that you will immediately need to compellingly articulate your worth to avoid being eliminated. We'll discuss this further in chapter 2, "Tell Me about Yourself." Start by identifying the qualities or characteristics that make you distinctive from the rest of your classmates. Be able to articulate *what you know* and *what you can do* for the company. Back up your statements with examples and stories directly from classroom experiences or from your part-time job, internship, or clinical experiences.

In an interview, your challenge is to bridge the gap between what you learned in school and how you can apply those skills in the job setting for the employer's benefit. Sometimes, hiring managers may not realize they need what you have to offer until you show them. This is called *selling value*. Employers need a reason, a benefit, or a gain for themselves, their department, or their company to hire you. They're not going to hire you just because you're a great person. And, to make matters more complicated, employers may or may not understand the value of your degree unless you explain it to them. By explaining how your training in accounting/biotech/human services can help the company uncover corporate fraud/ develop a new nanotech application/help returning Iraq War veterans adjust to civilian life, you are showing them how you can help the company get ahead, make a profit, reduce work, gain an edge, or remediate a problem. The graduates who can effectively articulate their value to the company usually win the job.

After the interview (and sometimes even *before* the interview) the top candidate(s) for the position will have their references checked, graduation dates verified, drug-testing results analyzed, and any other mandatory requirements completed. Some companies will check references themselves, or hire a third party to complete the background search for them. It is worth noting that many companies are now checking credit ratings and Twitter and Facebook accounts as part of their preemployment background checks. One company, Social Intelligence in Santa Barbara, California, specializes in conducting Internet background checks that are compliant with the Fair Credit Reporting Act.[7] When a search turns up evidence that might be used to deny an applicant credit (or a job), the act requires that employers notify applicants they are in danger of being disqualified and state the evidence on which disqualification would be based. The applicant then has five days to dispute the finding. This is just a preview of what's to come. Some people are predicting that Internet background checking will become automated using sophisticated methods like facial recognition software to verify authenticity on social media sites.

Once the background checks are completed, and assuming that no one has uncovered any skeletons buried in your background, the company will extend an offer and the discussion of salary and benefits will commence.

THE WAITING GAME

Unfortunately, in today's busy age you may not even get a response that your application was received until you're contacted to schedule an interview. This is especially true if you apply online where you have no contact with a live person whatsoever. HR offices have undergone downsizing like everyone else and are extremely pressed for time. That's why many companies now use applicant-tracking systems to sort, accept, or reject the thousands of resumes and applications they receive each day. The software works by scanning your resume for particular keywords. If your resume contains no "matches," it basically sits in a file on a server and ends up in the "cyberspace black hole" with all of the other resumes.

Despite the reality of our modern job application system, you should be diligent about trying to acquire a contact name. Then stay on top of those job applications and follow up every two to four weeks while you continue to look for new openings. Make follow-up calls and visits, because when new listings come out, some HR managers do not go through previous applicants. Continue to keep in touch until someone has been hired or the position is no longer open. This is when keeping a job search log comes in handy. It's easy to forget who you called when, and after a couple of weeks of searching (yes, it may take that long and even longer) things have a way of blurring together.

If you applied for a job and haven't heard back from a hiring manager, it is perfectly acceptable to contact him or her. Wait at least two weeks and then contact the manager and say something like, "Good morning, Mr. Jackson. My name is Susan Smith. Thank you for taking my call. I applied for xyz position about 14 days ago and have not heard a response. I just wanted to call and make sure you received my resume."

If the hiring manager did receive your resume or application, then this will be confirmed, and as a bonus, you'll probably learn the status of the hiring process. If he or she did not receive your resume, offer to send a new one.

Keep in mind that an employer's time is not your time. Employers are not waiting by the phone for a job offer like you are—they have meetings to attend, budgets to deal with, and a host of other issues that may take precedence over filling a position. What's unavailable to the job seeker during this time is the knowledge that something may have occurred on the employer's end that caused the process to be delayed.

Private companies and institutions will respond quicker than public or state agencies. Many state agencies are unable to advertise an opening until the incumbent leaves the position, and many allow four to six weeks for applicants to submit their materials. The search process at my college can be as long as six months by the time a search committee is formed, the required three levels of interviews conducted, references checked, and final board of trustees approval process completed.

Here are some tips to increase the chances of successfully finding a job in any kind of economy:

- *Start yesterday.* Do not wait until you graduate to begin looking for a position. Ideally, you should begin your job search four to six months ahead of time. Many recruiters begin recruiting in the fall semester, especially at larger universities. In a tight job market, it may take longer than anticipated to find a position, so you need to be available to interview when the jobs are posted, not just when it's convenient for you.

- *Actively search for jobs.* Do not simply wait for job openings to appear in the newspaper, or just passively click "apply" on job search engines. Go beyond the technology. Approach companies you may be interested in working for and inquire about possible openings. Use online sources like CareerBuilder.com, Indeed.com, and Dice.com; the newspaper classifieds; websites of professional organizations; and the classified sections in trade or professional journals. Identify the types of jobs you are interested in and the employers you want to target by looking in the phone book, at company websites, at the chamber of commerce, at professional organizations, or in business and industry directories.

Watch for "help wanted" signs. Ask friends, neighbors, professors, and working professionals in the field to help you locate possible job openings. Attend all job fairs in your area, and register with your local One-Stop Career Center, your local college career services, or a staffing or employment agency. Join your local alumni association or a local professional organization in your career field.

- *When you see a job opening, don't wait until next week to apply.* Apply immediately. One nursing recruiter told me that they get so many responses to their openings on CareerBuilder that they stop taking applications after five days. Create job alerts to notify you by e-mail of relevant job openings. If you see an opening that was posted several weeks ago, don't just assume that it has been filled. Try to contact the company and inquire if the job is still available.

- *Use LinkedIn, Facebook, or Twitter* to seek out recruiters, search for job openings, or connect with people who may know of job openings. Visit the employment section on company websites and then call or e-mail the HR office and inquire about openings. Send or give them a copy of your resume if they express an interest.

- *Customize your resume to individual job openings.* Stress your skills and results on your resume. Highlight the accomplishments you have accrued over your work history. If you returned to school to make a career change, highlight experience gained during clinicals, practica, student teaching, internships, research projects, or other related activities. On your resume, use a summary of your past accomplishments and expertise, rather than an employment objective.

- *Be organized.* Create a log and write down who you contacted. Include the date, the name of the company, the result of your contact, and the follow-up action needed or taken. Continue to follow up with each employer every two to four weeks as appropriate.

- *Bring a portfolio* to the interview to illustrate your skills by providing sample lesson plans, journalism articles, art projects, engineering designs, research papers, marketing or sales promotions, business proposals, honors or awards received, and/or employee evaluations. Strongly articulate your value to an employer. Confidently, professionally, and succinctly answer interview questions. Be able to answer the "Why should I hire you?" question. Follow up after an interview to express interest.

- *Conduct your job search in a formal, professional manner.* Dress, behave, and speak in a professional manner. Avoid using e-mail emoticons, writing or speaking in casual text messaging lingo, or wearing an outfit to an interview that is better suited for an evening with friends. That goes double for your voice-mail messages, e-mail addresses, and Facebook profile. Google yourself to view your profile as an employer would.

In my experience, the students who successfully find jobs are those who are proactive in their job search. They actively seek out openings, rather than waiting for jobs to come to them.

TWO

Tell Me about Yourself

Knowing others is wisdom, knowing yourself is enlightenment.

—Lao Tzu

"Tell me about yourself" is one of the most common, and most difficult, questions interviewees face. An employer will often use this question as an "ice-breaker" during the initial minutes of the interview, but it is not a social question. So please don't tell them about your relationship status, what movies you saw, or what hobbies you enjoy. What the employer really wants to know is if you have the educational background, skills, and work experience that they are looking for in a candidate. The problem is that most students, when faced with this question, are often totally unprepared and usually end up stammering, "Uhhhh . . . " (*not* the right answer).

The "Tell me about yourself" question is a test—a test of your preparedness for the interview and of your ability to summarize your educational background, relevant work experience, and personal abilities to the employer. Ultimately, it's a test of how well you can sell yourself.

The answer to "Tell me about yourself," just like any other answer provided during an interview, should always be focused on your education background, your skills and knowledge, and your past experience—and, ultimately, on how these will benefit the employer. In other words: work and school. The proper response is to provide a summary of where you are in your educational career, a few highlights about your strengths or qualifications, and any other tidbits of information that will round out your desirability as a candidate.

Let's look at some examples:

Poor answer: "Well, I just turned 21, enjoy sky diving, and have over 600 friends on Facebook." While this may be is a great answer in any other social situation, it unfortunately tells the employer absolutely nothing about why they should hire you.

Better answer: "I will be graduating with a bachelor's degree in communications with a minor in web design from Famous State University this May. During my fall semester I completed a 20-hour-a-week internship at XYZ Communications in which I designed and maintained their social media website."

In this example, the response provided the answers to:

1. *Who* you are and your current situation
2. *What* you have accomplished

Become comfortable with certain talking points, such as:

- What you know about the industry and the company, and how it relates to your education and experience
- The aspects of the potential new job that you're excited about
- How your skills will fit the position
- Your ambitions and accomplishments in a relevant manner
- And anything about your personality that is applicable to the job (leader, team player, enjoy research, etc.)

Here's a good example of a well-thought-out response:

I've been interested in chemistry since high school. In college I was able to work with Dr. Lazarus in his research on polymers. In my internship with Idea Corporation, I was able to successfully take what I learned in the classroom and apply it to my laboratory projects. I enjoy team projects and have successfully led some of these projects. I'm very proud of the honors our chemistry team earned during the U.S. National Chemistry Olympiad Competition last year.

Everything I've read about your company and what I've learned about the position during this interview has only reinforced my desire to work here. I'm very focused and I believe I have what it takes to be successful in this position.

Your response has now provided the perfect invitation for the employer to ask in more detail about your internships and past training.

Avoid opening the door to any shortcomings. Don't use statements like, "I've learned from my mistakes ...," or "After I struggled with my previous major ... " Statements like that will only lead to follow-up questions that may put you on the defensive.

30-SECOND SELF-MARKETING STATEMENT

You can use the first part of your response to the "Tell me about yourself" question to formulate your 30-second self-marketing statement, also known as the "elevator pitch." A good way to understand the concept of the elevator pitch is to imagine you are getting on an elevator, you meet a potential recruiter or employer, and you have only 15 seconds to convey who you are and impress him or her enough to warrant a further conversation. In other words, you've got to convey "who you are, why you're interested, why you're qualified, and what can you do for them" in 30 seconds or less. Sounds simple, right?

Four items make up a complete self-marketing statement:

1. Who you are (your educational background and relevant work experience)
2. Why you're qualified (*how* your education, knowledge, skills, and accomplishments can benefit the company)
3. What you can do for them (one or two specific areas in which you can help the company)
4. Why you're interested (you're inquiring about possible job openings)

Here is an example of a complete self-marketing statement:

Good morning. My name is Donna Smith. I'll be graduating with a bachelor's degree in communications this May. During my fall semester I completed a 20-hour a week internship at XYZ Communications setting up their social media website. I would like to work for your company to improve the effectiveness of your social networking website and was wondering if you have any job openings?

Other closing variations are:

"May I give you a copy of my resume?"

"What are you looking for in an employee?" (This opens the conversation further.)

"Can I schedule a few minutes of your time to discuss opportunities with your company?"

You can use the self-marketing statement in any setting where you have a limited audience with the recruiter/employer such as during a job fair, in a cover letter, during a casual networking conversation, or in a Twitter post.

IDENTIFYING SKILLS

Giving a potential employer examples of skills that can help them implies that (1) you are aware of what skills you possess, and (2) you know what skills and knowledge employers value.

Let's use an example to help you look at yourself from an employer's perspective. Think about the last time you went to the dentist. What did you like (or not like) about your experience? Was your hygienist nice? Rough? Competent? Friendly? Impatient? If your experience was unpleasant, would you return?

To make your dental experience a pleasant one, most dentists would like their dental hygienists to have the following qualities:

1. *Customer service*: This means having the ability to build relationships with clients and keep them coming back, be empathetic and kind, and providing them with information they need. Most clients are afraid of going to the dentist. At the very least, they may not be afraid but they go to the dentist only because they have to or it's good for them. So think about it: You come into the dentist office for your cleaning appointment; maybe you're really not looking forward to it and you are greeted by a crabby, impatient hygienist. What are the chances that you're going to come back again? Probably nil. I know I wouldn't. However, if you are treated by someone pleasant, kind, who maybe makes you laugh and feel more comfortable, you're probably going to come back again.

2. *Skills and knowledge*: This would include being schooled in proper dental hygiene techniques, familiar with dental equipment, and competent in cleaning teeth according to professional guidelines with minimal discomfort, as well as having the ability to keep and maintain records accurately.

3. *Soft skills*: These include the ability to work independently, be reliable, come in to work on time, and conduct oneself in a professional

manner. A bonus would be an employee who can learn new techniques quickly and has an eagerness to help out and take on new responsibilities when needed.

Why does the employer concern themselves with these things? Because the bottom line is that the dentist (and any other employer) is in business to provide a quality service. That's how they make money. In a service industry (which is what dentistry is) repeat customers are the mainstay of their business. And who helps the dentist retain customers? The staff, of course. As a member of that staff, the dental hygienist who delivers high-quality dental hygiene services, in a professional and pleasant manner, will keep customers coming back again.

In an interviewing situation, the dentist is trying to determine which candidate will be the best person to fill that role. So the dentist is going to hire the person who best fits the dentist's idea of the perfect dental hygienist.

If you were a dental hygienist searching for a job, and you knew this information ahead of time, you would know which professional skills and personal qualities to emphasize during the interview. The same line of reasoning can be used when applying for a position in any other major or career field.

Now, it's your turn. Write down your unique skills and attributes using these three areas as a guide:

1. Knowledge
2. Skills (soft and technical)
3. Personal traits/characteristics that you possess

Most people either have a hard time coming up with a list of accomplishments and skills, or underestimate their abilities and accomplishments. I usually ask students to make a list of what they've accomplished since they've been enrolled in college. Another good exercise is to ask yourself how your friends might describe you—are you a leader, team player, smart, creative, detail oriented, organized? These are all good words to describe what you can bring to the work setting.

Ask your friends or family to help you create your list by asking them what they like best about you. You'll find that other people will have no problem rattling off your accomplishments (and your strengths and weaknesses). You may even receive some surprising answers. Whether you like (or don't like) what you hear, someone else's perspective is crucial to helping you move closer to viewing yourself through the eyes of an employer. You may also begin to realize what you do have to offer and how valuable you really are!

IT'S NOT BRAGGING

Most of us were taught not to brag. How many of you are annoyed by someone who is always talking about how great they are or how well they did in something? No one wants to hear someone monopolize a conversation by talking about themselves because it is usually overdone or said at the wrong time and under the wrong circumstances.

But it's not bragging to talk about yourself in the interview. The interview *is* the appropriate place and time to talk about yourself.

If you tend to be on the shy side, practice a few statements ahead of time in front of a mirror. The way I like to view it is that I am "simply stating the facts."

Practice calmly and matter-of-factly, outlining your abilities in an even, confident tone: "I have above-average skills in _____, and feel that I am very good at (doing) _____." It is always helpful to back up your statements with examples from work or school activities.

This exercise will help you answer the last question that is often asked in an interview: "Why should I hire you?" In some way, shape, or form, an employer will be trying to discover the answer to that question during your interview, so don't let the employer guess—spell it out.

WRITING A LINKEDIN SUMMARY

A LinkedIn summary is unique. It is not really a resume and it's not quite a blog. Unlike a resume, your LinkedIn summary can be longer, more creative, and written in first person ("I").

Lindsay Pollack, best-selling author, speaker, and spokesperson for LinkedIn, says that your LinkedIn summary statement should resemble the first few paragraphs of your best-written cover letter.[1] Even though you can write in first person, the content of your summary should still focus on the professional. Take care not to be too familiar, conversational, or unprofessional. Sounds complicated, doesn't it? It is. You can use some of the language from your resume summary or your self-marketing pitch to write a LinkedIn summary or vice versa.

When writing your summary, consider your audience. Who are you trying to appeal to? Employers? Recruiters? Other professionals in your career field? If you are looking for a job, then you may want pretend that you are writing directly to your future employer. After all, LinkedIn *is* the appropriate place to promote yourself.

Keep these four questions in mind as you formulate your summary:

1. Who are you? (Use adjectives like *creative, dynamic.*)
2. What do you want to do in the future? (Make a general statement.)
3. What have you done recently in your major? (Use specific, relevant examples.)
4. What do you have to offer an employer? (Write from the viewpoint of what you can do for them, not what they can do for you.)

Here are some examples of well-written LinkedIn summaries:

Creative graphic design graduate with a passion for producing high-quality work. Fluent in English, Spanish, and Portuguese. Technically proficient in Quark Xpress and all Adobe products (Illustrator, Photoshop, InDesign, and Acrobat). Interested in helping a company create a strong online presence by incorporating graphic design techniques into web-based advertising.

I am a nursing student who will be graduating in May from Luzerne County Community College. I have completed rotations in pediatrics, med/surg, psychiatry, and community health. My professors have described me as empathetic, patient oriented, and dedicated to delivering quality nursing care. I am scheduled to take the Pennsylvania state nursing exam in July.

THREE

Create a Results-Based, Value-Added Resume

Man is always more than he can know of himself; consequently, his accomplishments, time and again, will come as a surprise to him.

—Henry Wadsworth Longfellow

The formula for successfully finding employment is quite simple: the closer your skills, education, and experience match the job description, the greater your chances are of being selected for the position. The resume is the first step in the job-hunting process to establish that connection.

We have all heard that employers take anywhere from 5 to 30 seconds to read a resume. The number of seconds doesn't really matter—the point is that the amount of time an employer spends looking at your resume is not very long. Employers are busy and most will initially scan through your resume to determine if your qualifications warrant another look. That means that if you want your resume to be included in the first screening, you'll need to prepare your resume in such a way that your important points are clearly and concisely stated and will be visible. That means using less "fluff" and more facts about your achievements. Use bullets to highlight achievements, and whenever possible, document your statements with real data.

The purpose of the resume is to be invited in for the interview. People are rarely (although it does occasionally happen) hired based just on their resume. Most employers want to see the candidate in person and verify that the statements on the resume are indeed accurate. What do employers look for in a resume? Beyond the candidate's ability to meet standard criteria—the "right" major or work experience—employers are most likely to look for evidence that the candidate is able to work in a team, according to a new survey conducted by NACE.[1] Nearly 80 percent of employers taking part in NACE's *Job Outlook 2012* survey said they search for evidence that the potential employee can work in a team, and more than three-quarters indicated they want the resume to show the candidate has leadership abilities and written communication skills. Evidence of problem-solving skills and a strong work ethic round out the top five "soft skills" employers seek on resumes.

In order to be successful in today's competitive job market, your resume and cover letter must be action-driven and clearly demonstrate the value you bring to a company. When describing relevant experience, you must describe *what* you did, *how* you did it, and what the *results* or *outcomes* were. Do not simply provide a list of duties performed. Use an action verb to describe the task and include the result (or "value added") to illustrate your contribution to the organization. Impress the reader with quantitative data such as number of students taught, employees supervised, percentage increase in profits or efficiency, number of units managed, number of sales calls completed, or number of customer complaints resolved.

Here are some examples: "Taught at-risk preschool children at two inner-city day care centers," "Organized the annual United Way awards ceremony," "Wrote a promotional sales flyer that increased sales by 14 percent," "Coordinated a fund-raising event that drew a record crowd of 1,200 people."

Some students write one good resume and then use it to apply to all openings. But the problem is that not all job openings are alike. Each position is unique depending on the needs of the company, the makeup of the position, and the skills and educational experience deemed necessary to carry out the job. A more effective way to approach your job search is to target your resume to each job description. Read the job description, identify key points, and customize your resume accordingly. Targeting or customizing resumes to individual job openings means that you'll have to create several versions of your resume, each one highlighting different experiences, skills, or accomplishments, depending on the requirements listed in the job description.

To target your resume to a particular job opening, carefully read the description and ask yourself the following questions:

1. What can be inferred from the job title?
2. What is the educational level required for the position?
3. Are there a required number of years of experience?

4. What are the job duties and responsibilities?
5. Are there any technical skills, particular software programs, or credentials required for the position?
6. Is there any technical jargon or occupation-specific terminology used in the job description ("just-in-time purchasing," "Microsoft Office applications," "Quark Xpress")?
7. Are there any required or preferred "soft skills"?

Then modify your resume so that it exactly matches the requirements listed in the job description. Keep in mind that *required* generally means you will not get the position unless you have those skills, but *preferred* means the employer will give preference to the candidate who has those skills. So make sure you include any "required" or "preferred" skills in your resume.

TRANSLATING COLLEGE EXPERIENCES TO WORK

Just because you don't have formal work experience during college does not mean that the Work Experience section of your resume has to remain blank. In lieu of professional work experience in your major, it is acceptable to list your clinical, internship, co-op, and practicum experiences as work-related experiences on your resume. Simply identify them accordingly such as an "internship," "field experience," or "clinical experience."

But don't stop there—use what else you did in college to show an employer what you can do on the job. Think about any organizations you belonged to, any committees you served on, or any volunteer or service learning experiences you completed. If you were the president of a club or your student government association, you may have organized fund-raisers, held meetings, prepared a budget, or written publicity articles for the local newspaper, all of which can be listed on your resume under the headings of Volunteer Experience, Community Activities, or Leadership. Involvement in extracurricular activities can show a potential employer that you have time management, project management, organizational, and multitasking skills. Involvement in clubs and organizations can also demonstrate some of those critical soft skills that employers are always looking for such as interpersonal skills, leadership, initiative, and teamwork.

Let's say you're the treasurer of your photography club. That experience probably helped you develop budgetary skills. Likewise, a leadership position in a club or organization can demonstrate leadership potential. If you're a college student in a state that was having budget cuts, you may have lobbied or organized a rally at your state capital against education cuts or tuition raises. This shows political action and organizational ability. Participating in a local cancer charity run/walk may have given you experience raising funds, coordinating volunteers, or soliciting donations—all of which can be transferred to the business or public relations setting. Your involvement in these types of activities during college helped you develop skills that can be directly transferred to a professional position and should be listed on your resume.

OBJECTIVES VERSUS CAREER SUMMARIES

Most of us were taught to use an objective when writing a resume. However, current career wisdom recommends using a *summary* or a *professional profile* rather than an objective.

One of the problems with using an objective is that it is often written in general terms that really add nothing to the resume. "Seeking an entry-level position with a respected company where I can use my education and background" doesn't add much value to your resume and tells the employer what *you* want, not what the employer wants.

Hiring personnel scan resumes to determine if applicants have the competencies and achievements to be successful in their position. A professional summary can capture this information in a couple of sentences, right at the top of the page. Think of the summary as a snapshot of your accomplishments. A good summary will allow you to match your skill set to the requirements listed in the job posting while still providing the flexibility of targeting your resume to a particular position.

There are other uses for a well-written career summary: it can be used as the basis for a response to the "Tell me about yourself" question so often asked in an interview, and as a starting point for a LinkedIn summary statement.

Following are some examples of summary statements:

Bachelor's degree student in exercise physiology with two years of high school coaching experience. Independent self-starter who has a passion for educating people about the benefits of a healthy lifestyle.

Mechanical engineering graduate with concentration in alternative energy. Areas of interest include using alternative fuels to improve fuel performance in automobiles. Completed a semester-long internship at XYZ Manufacturing focusing on using new biotech alternative fuel sources.

Full-time electronics engineering technology student. Seeking part-time employment in my field while I finish my degree. I am a dedicated worker who will go above expectations and will be a great asset to the company willing to offer me an opportunity.

RESUME LANGUAGE

Resumes have a writing style that is unique unto itself. Resume language uses words and phrases that concisely describe your skills and work duties in a way that will be noticed by the employer. Generally speaking, job-related skills are written in the form of an action verb in the resume. Examples of skills are: *educate, design, create, coach, sell, market, advertise, manage, train, evaluate, repair, install, and inspect.*

Adding a noun after the verb creates a descriptive phrase. Examples are: *assessed learning, diagnosed illness, coordinated an advertising campaign, produced a television show, administered tests, mediated differences*, and *resolved complaints.* These phrases (written in sentence or bulleted format) are usually included in the Work Experience section.

To make your statements more results or achievement oriented, add adjectives to your descriptive phrase: *resolved customer complaints, trained 10 employees, mediated differences between labor and management, created an award-winning documentary*, and *taught developmental reading to entering college freshmen.* See how these phrases add value, highlight accomplishments, and yet are concise?

Today, many large companies use applicant-tracking software to match resumes with open positions via *keywords. Keywords* and *keyword phrases* are terminology or jargon that is specific to your profession (usually nouns). Examples of occupation-specific keyword phrases are: "Microsoft Office proficient," "AutoCAD 2011," "chairside dental assisting," or "Cisco Management." Use keywords to highlight your accomplishments in the Summary, Skills, or Employment sections of your resume. If a company is seeking a position with specific skills or qualifications, the software will automatically select all of the resumes that include those words or phrases.

THE COMPONENTS OF THE RESUME

1. *Name*: Contact information. I like to center the contact information and write my name in a 24-point font to make it noticeable. It has been suggested that in our online age, street addresses will no longer

be necessary, only e-mail addresses and cell phone numbers. But until then, I would include your complete contact information in your resume.

Example:

Jason A. Jones

1234 South Popular Street   jajones@aol.com
Anytown, USA 53789   507.740.01234

2. *Career Summary*: Summarize your educational background, graduation status, and skills and experience.

Example:

Dedicated and accomplished music graduate with solid academic background in music theory and performance in voice and piano. Member of the university a cappella ensemble. Eligible for a Pennsylvania teaching license.

3. *Education*: New graduates should begin their resume with the Education section. Education is your most saleable feature. After you have been working for a couple of years, you can move the Education section down to the bottom of the resume and put your Work Experience section at the top.

Example:

University of Wisconsin, Madison, Wisconsin
Bachelor of Science degree in Biology, Business Management Minor, 2011
4.0 GPA, Magna Cum Laude

Note that "associate degree" is singular (not *associates* degree); however, "bachelor's degree" and "master's degree" are possessives.

If you have not yet graduated, indicate this by writing, "Expected graduation May 2012."

List your GPA only if above 3.0.

4. *Awards*: Include dean's list, president's list, honor societies, contests won, or any honorable mentions or citations awarded. If you do not have any awards, then skip this section.

Example:

Dean's list, Fall 2010, Spring 2011
First-place award in Valley Journalism contest, 2011

5. *Skills*: Bullet or list any technical skills you have such as software programs or equipment.

6. *Work Experience*: List work experience in reverse chronological order (current to past). Related work experience may be separated from nonrelated work experience. Internships, clinicals, practica, student teaching, or fieldwork can also be included under Experience and are titled as such.

   Start each sentence with an action-oriented verb such as *achieved, assembled, assisted, coordinated, evaluated, improved, managed, performed, produced, researched, sold, supervised,* and *trained.* Avoid phrases such as "responsible for" or "duties included," which can create a passive tone. Instead, use active verbs to describe what you actually did, such as, "Wrote and designed flyers and brochures for new products," or "Developed a new sales brochure."

   If you are currently at a position, write the date as "2011–present" and the verbs in *present tense (provide, train, assemble,* and *package).* If you are no longer at the position, the verbs should be written in *past tense (provided, trained, assembled,* and *packaged).*

7. *Organizations*: List any student or professional organizations that you belong to.

   Example:

   President, Student Government Association, Fall 2011

8. *Languages* (if applicable): For bilingual speakers or green card holders.

   Example:

   Native Russian (permanent resident) or Bilingual in xxx and yyy

9. *Other sections* (as applicable): In the Washington, DC, area it is not unusual to see headings of Citizenship and Visa Status on resumes.

10. *Community Activities*: List any activities you have participated in outside of school such as study abroad, membership in community-based clubs or organizations, coaching or athletic activities, art or music contests, volunteer activities, fund-raising or charitable events, etc.

OVERALL FORMAT

Follow these rules to create an attractive, organized, and easy-to-read resume:

- It should be only one page in length.
- Margins should be one inch.

- Use either Times New Roman 12-point font, Calibri 11-point font, or Arial 10-point font.
- Avoid fancy fonts, graphics, or features (unless you're in a creative field such as graphic design—and then your resume *is* your portfolio).
- Avoid using too much underlining or italics (this may be distracting). Use caps or the bold feature for header emphasis.
- Use the consistency rule—which says your formatting style should be consistent throughout your resume (e.g., if you bold one header in a section, bold all headers).

See Appendix A for more examples of resumes.

COVER LETTERS

A cover letter introduces yourself to the employer and gives the reader a taste of what is to be found in the resume. It should be professional yet friendly, and convey competence. Think of the cover letter as your way of beginning a conversation with the employer. It should be short and to the point, clearly stating your purpose for writing, and summarizing your key experiences, skills, and accomplishments.

Writing a cover letter is more difficult than it initially appears. I recommend preparing several drafts, enlisting the input of others, and refining your letter until it is perfect. The cover letter displays not only your knowledge and skills to an employer but also your communication skills. Make sure your grammar, spelling, and punctuation are flawless!

I really like this suggestion for new grads from Job-Hunt.org: "Frame your experience so that it aligns with what the employer needs. Avoid writing a cover letter that restates your entire history. Instead say, 'I understand you are looking for X. My experience with X includes . . .' "

Always use some version of a cover letter (see the following guidelines) when applying for a position:

- When applying for an advertised position in the newspaper, or when the employer specifically requests applicants to apply by mail, it is appropriate to use a traditional, paper cover letter.
- If you are sending your resume to an employer via e-mail, use an electronic cover letter (e-letter). An e-letter is written in the body of the e-mail, preferably at the top of the e-mail (but not sent as an attachment), and is short and direct. E-letters are quickly replacing

traditional cover letters as more and more employers are accepting resumes by e-mail.

- If you are faxing your resume to an employer, include a brief cover letter with your resume (you can use your e-letter).

Some Cover Letter Don'ts

Don't address the letter "Dear Sirs." Not only will you offend the reader if she happens to be a woman, but it shows that you haven't taken the time to do your research. Instead, find out the name of the person who will be reviewing your resume by contacting the company's HR department. If no contact information was given, try searching the company's website on the Internet. Look for the "About Us" section or the company directory. If all else fails and you are unable to obtain a name, address your letter "Attention: Human Resources Department."

Don't send a cover letter that has not been thoroughly proofread. Typographical and grammatical errors (such as confusing "you're" with "your") create a poor impression and may be used to weed out candidates.

Don't send a generic letter. You can make a much better impression by mentioning the company name and doing a little research so you can say something intelligent about the company. Research what the company produces, or prides themselves on, by checking their website.

Don't forget to state which position you are applying for. Many companies advertise multiple positions at a time.

REFERENCES

References typically fall into two categories: personal and professional. Professional references are preferable as they give a potential employer the ability to confirm your work history. Personal references work well for those with little work history. The important thing to remember is that both types of references can, and will, be checked.

Do not include references at the bottom of the resume, and do not send them to an employer unless specifically requested to do so. Instead of writing "references available upon request," bring in a professionally prepared list of three to five references that you can hand to the employer during the interview. Having the list in your portfolio ready to present when asked shows your preparation and your professionalism. The exception to this rule is when applying for government positions. Always include your references at the bottom of your resume when you're applying for a state or federal government position.

The following are some useful tips on references:

1. *Choose your references wisely.* Select people who will say positive things about you and your ability to work and be successful. Do not select friends, coworkers, or family members. Current and former employers/supervisors, professors/instructors, or advisors are acceptable as well as people in positions of authority who you worked with on volunteer or community-based projects.

2. *Ask permission first.* Make sure you have the approval of your reference before you use his or her name. You don't want your star reference to say "Susie *Who?*" or stumble around for something nice to say in response to a recruiter's reference-checking phone call.

3. *Coach your references.* This will probably not be necessary if you are using someone familiar with your abilities, such as a professor or clinical/research supervisor. However, it doesn't hurt to tell them about any activities that you're involved in outside of their purview or to provide them with additional details such as new accomplishments or awards.

4. *Inform your references about potential calls.* Whenever possible, tell your references who will be calling them and when to expect the call. Your references will be better prepared to sell you and your abilities if they are prepared.

5. *Periodically update your references on the status of your job search.* When you do get a job, let your references know and thank them for their support. If it has been over a year and you are still looking for work, check to make sure they are still willing to be a reference. Remember, they are doing you a favor by consenting to be a reference!

Keep in mind that at many companies former employers are allowed to confirm only employment dates and salary history. So make sure you use a reference who can provide the type of information that you want conveyed concerning your work history and ethics.

SUBMITTING YOUR RESUME TO AN EMPLOYER

1. *Traditional mail:* Submitting a resume via mail is occurring less and less. In the event you do need to mail your resume, include a cover letter, but don't staple them together.

2. *E-mail*: The subject line is the first point of contact. Many unsolicited e-mails end up in the spam folder because they contain punctuation like exclamation points or blank subject lines. Don't assume that the employer knows why they are receiving your resume. I get resumes all the time with empty subject lines or no explanation other than "Resume." I don't know whether to edit, post, or trash them. Then I have to spend time e-mailing the student and waiting for a response. Employers are not going to do that. So be clear about what position you are applying for and write "Mary Jones Resume" or "Dental Hygiene Position" in the subject line.

3. *Fax*: Include a fax cover sheet with a brief explanation and state the position you're applying for. Watch for spelling and grammatical errors!

4. *Online*: When asked to submit your resume online, type it in plain-text format. Even though some databases are able to upload a resume prepared in a Word document, they will still convert it to a plain-text file for posting. The design of an electronic resume is different from a traditional paper-and-pencil format. Include relevant keywords in a separate section or in your summary. Do not use bold, italics, underline, shading, graphics, parentheses, or horizontal lines because they do not translate well into applicant tracking systems.

RESUME TRENDS

- *Keep it short.* Ten years ago, resumes were two, three, or four pages long, showcasing a candidate's qualifications, achievements, and more. Today's resumes, however, must be short and should span only one page for new graduates. The exception is if you're an adult student with previous work experience—then you may extend the resume to two pages. The modern resume must still incorporate qualifications, value, and accomplishments, but it's simply written tighter, cleaner, and leaner. Shorten two sentences to one. Eliminate an extra bullet point. Summarize all of the technical skills into one line.

- *Delete "References available upon request."* It is no longer necessary to state "references available upon request" at the bottom of the resume anymore—it's implied.

- *Keep it employer focused.* Today's resumes must be focused on what employers are looking for in candidates, not what job seekers want. Today's resumes often incorporate graphics, logos, text boxes, borders, or shading to make them more noticeable. But these enhancements are usually appropriate only for graduates in the creative arts professions who want to demonstrate their design talent. However, a tasteful use of borders or shading can provide a competitive edge for all job seekers.

- *Use Word or a PDF format.* Microsoft Word is the dominant global word processing software and is the standard that most applicant-tracking systems are built upon. That makes it imperative that you create your resume in a Word (.doc or .docx) format, or if you do not have Word, convert it to a pdf file. Be aware that not everyone has adopted the latest Word format (e.g., .docx in Word 2010), so you may want to save your resume in a lower-level .doc format to ensure that readers will be able to open and read your resume. Plain-text versions (saved as .txt) still remain the best format to use when pasting resumes into online job applications.

If you are active on Twitter, you can use http://www.TwitRes.com to display your resume. All you need to do is upload a copy of your print resume and it will appear as the background on their Twitter page. Video resumes, interactive resumes, and infographic resumes are the hot, new resume trends on the horizon. If you're applying for a job that requires creativity, innovative thinking, or problem solving, one way to make yourself stand out is through a unique digital resume. Keep in mind that creative resume formats are received better in certain industries such as marketing, public relations, sales, advertising, journalism, graphic design, social media, and communications.

Adding hyperlinks to direct the reader to a webpage, e-portfolio, or other information is becoming more popular, especially for graduates in art and communication fields. A single hyperlink typed under the contact information is another way to direct readers to relevant information. Keep in mind that hyperlinks are not very compatible with applicant tracking software, so only use hyperlinks when you are sending your resume by e-mail.

FOUR

Where to Look for Job Openings

Finding the right work is like discovering your own soul in the world.

—Thomas Moore

One of the underemphasized aspects of job searching is where to look for job openings. In a good economy, when there are many job openings, graduates do not have to look any farther than their college's annual recruiting event or job fair. But in a tough economy, where there are more applicants than there are positions, graduates need to expand their search beyond the borders of their career center to find openings.

After College surveyed 1,450 college graduates and alumni from March to April 2011. When they looked at the methods used by graduates who reported that they had a moderate to very easy time finding work, these were the results[1]:

- 70.5 percent of respondents applied directly to the company or organization, and 62 percent applied to job boards.
- Tied at 60.3 percent were attending a school career fair and speaking to someone who already works at the company.
- 53.4 percent spoke to friends and family members.
- 49.1 percent attended an on-campus information session.
- 49.1 percent spoke to a professor/teacher/dean.
- 47.4 percent contacted a recruiter.
- 34.2 percent visited the career center.

- 23.9 percent networked at an association or club.
- 19.7 percent used a social networking site.
- 7.7 percent blogged about issues that pertained to their career interest.

What does all of this tell us? Although networking and word-of-mouth referrals are reported as the number one way to find jobs for job seekers in general, it appears that the best methods for college graduates are right in their school—at career fairs and employer information sessions, where employers are specifically looking to hire you.

Here are some additional places to look for job openings:

1. Public employment services such as your One-Stop Career Center, your local chamber of commerce, and community job-posting sites
2. Internet job boards, job search engines, company websites, and websites for specific industries or occupations (niche job boards)
3. College or university career offices and alumni organizations
4. Women's centers and community-based career services for people who belong to a particular "special populations" category, such as single parents, displaced homemakers, or members of an underrepresented group based on gender or ethnicity
5. Trade magazines and professional organizations
6. Employer directories such as Standard and Poor's Register of Public Companies, Hoover's online, Business.com, or geographically based directories like the Job Bank series
7. Job or career fairs in your local or regional geographic area
8. Executive recruiters or employment agencies (also called staffing or personnel agencies) (When using these agencies, find out whether they charge you, or the employer, a fee for their services.)

USING CLASSIFIED ADS

Despite the popularity of job boards and Internet search engines, many jobs are still advertised in the newspaper. Unlike the college system of majors and minors that you are used to, the job market is organized by industry and job function. Examples of *industries* are health care, finance, education, engineering, and manufacturing. Examples of *job functions* or *job families* are teaching, accounting, managing, and counseling. To get an idea of how the job market is organized, just look at the classified section of any newspaper. Some of the major job categories or industries that hire employees are: *automotive, administration, clerical, customer service, education, general labor, health care, management, manufacturing, professional, retail, restaurant, sales, skilled, unskilled,* and *trade.*

So, if you're an education major, you'll want to look for newspaper ads in the Education section (although you could find relevant positions under Sales—e.g., educational sales). But if you are a business major, you could look under Administration, Customer Service, Management, Professional, Retail, or Sales, depending on your major and your career interests. Liberal arts majors, depending on your interests and skill set, could potentially find positions in almost any category of the classifieds.

USING JOB BOARDS

Job boards have become increasingly popular in recent years. One of the main attractions is that they are easy to use—just upload your resume and press "Apply." The problem with job boards is they may receive thousands of hits each day for a single opening. And that is why fewer than 5 percent of job seekers find jobs through these sites alone.

The other problem with job boards is that job listings may be duplicates, outdated, or scams. Users often find that posting a resume on the major job boards results in a flood of e-mails advertising get-rich-quick, multi-level marketing, and pyramid schemes, or calls from recruiters for jobs that you're not interested in.

Some job boards have very rigid requirements for how your resume or profile must be set up if it is to be posted on their site, so it can be hard to make your credentials stand out. A final disadvantage to using job boards is that it may be difficult to follow up after responding to a job posting because you do not have access to the name of the company or the hiring manager.

Given all of the drawbacks to job boards, they still are a very useful job search tool. How do you decide which job board to use? Chris Russell, CEO/founder of AllCountyJobs.com LLC, offers these tips[2]:

How to Spot a Good Job Board

There are thousands of job boards to choose from if you need to post a job. But not all are created equal. Here are some telltale signs that the job board you are about to post on is worth using.

1. **It Looks Good:** If the job board has good design, meaning a nice logo and well done interface with clearly spelled out call to actions and navigation.

2. **Contact Info:** If the job board puts their phone and email in a prominent place on the page. This means they're not afraid to be contacted. I always put my phone number at the top of every page of my sites.

3. **Too Much Backfill:** Many job boards these days backfill their listings with [jobs from other job search engines]. There's nothing wrong with this as it provides an additional source of revenue for them. But beware of sites that don't have any original listings.

4. **Outdated blog:** Many boards run their own blogs. If that blog hasn't been updated recently, watch out. It's a sign the job board is dying.

5. **Does it Google Well:** Do a keyword search for that job board based on its name or niche. If it doesn't appear in the first 1–2 pages of results, chances are the site doesn't get much traffic.

6. **Do They Syndicate:** This is not a total deal breaker since many sites can stand on their own for traffic. But see if your job board also syndicates to the major aggregators. If they do that means you get more than you are paying for. It's like getting multiple sites for 1 price.

7. **Age:** How long has your job board been around. The older it's been online the more likely it is to be worthy of your jobs.

Reprinted by permission of Chris Russell, http://www.recruitingblogs .com/profiles/blogs/how-to-spot-a-good-job-board.

The big job boards, such as Monster or CareerBuilder, are a good starting place for an Internet job search because they access a wide variety of jobs. Websites like Indeed.com, Jobster.com, or SimplyHired use spider technology to pull openings from other job boards.

To make the maximum use of job boards, it's helpful to find an inside company contact *before* you apply. Gerry Crispin, SPHR and principal at CareerXRoads.com, a consulting firm, suggests typing in the company name and the name of your school on LinkedIn to find connections at that company.

Adding widgets, gadgets, apps, and tools like job alerts can really expedite your job search, and there are a variety of job search apps available for your iPhone, iPad, or tablet. You can download apps that search for jobs by keyword and location (using the iPhone GPS function), e-mail job listings, keep track of your contacts, and even create a resume. Most of these apps are free and are provided by Indeed.com, LinkedIn, Facebook, LinkUp, Monster.com, Beyond.com, CareerBuilder.com,

TwitterFon, and JobServe, just to name a few. Other apps can be purchased for a reasonable fee but you may want to check their reviews before you buy.

NICHE JOB BOARD SITES

Many employers prefer to post positions on sites devoted to their industry, often called *niche* sites. An example of an industry-specific search engine for IT professionals is Dice.com. There are even niche job boards for applicants who belong to a minority group or specialized population such as women in trades or students with disabilities.

Small- or mid-size-business owners, in particular, generally have more luck finding a qualified resource through a site that is specific to, let's say, engineers in the Chicago area, rather than on a major job board that caters to all types of job seekers nationwide. If you are in a specialized major, versus a generalized major like liberal arts, you're going to have more success focusing your energies on industry-specific recruiters or niche job boards rather than generalized job boards that cater to everyone.

A Google search can usually bring up any job boards specific to your major or even to your hometown. The CareerOneStop website at http://www.careeronestop.org also provides a searchable database of niche job boards. Targeted industry listings can also be found on the websites of professional associations and societies, such as the Software Contractors Guild or the American Institute of Certified Public Accountants.[3]

Here are some examples of niche job markets:

Accounting and Finance Jobs (http://www.accountingprofessional.com): A job board for jobs in accounting and finance; thousands of jobs posted directly by employers and by recruiters

The Ad Club Job Board (http://theadclubevents.org/jobboard): Local jobs in advertising and a good source for news and events

AllCountyJobs.com (http://www.allcountyjobs.com): A collection of local and industry-specific job boards from Washington, DC, to Boston

American Marketing Association–Boston (http://amaboston.org): Marketing jobs in the Boston, Massachusetts, area

Dice (http://www.dice.com): A premier source of employment for IT professionals.

Hcareers (http://www.hcareers.com): Positions in the hospitality industry.

JobsInLogistics.com (http://www.JobsInLogistics.com): Positions in distribution, logistics, supply chain, freight forwarding, 3PL, purchasing and manufacturing

COMPANY WEBSITES

One way to avoid third-party job postings is, of course, to apply for jobs directly through company career sites. For many majors, finding appropriate company websites will be the most productive way to spend your time. Search engines like LinkUp, for example, pull jobs from company websites and automatically update their list when jobs are added or deleted from company websites.

The results of the AfterCollege survey reflect the trend that companies are placing more emphasis on beefing up their corporate career sites to attract job seekers.[4] An analysis of hiring data by Jobs2web Inc. found that to make one hire, recruiters wade through more than six times as many applications from job boards than they do from their own websites. According to the analysis, companies look through about 219 applications per job from job seekers who discovered the posting on a major board, such as Monster.com or CareerBuilder.com, before finding someone to hire, compared with 33 applications per hire from job hunters who find the job on the company's own career site and 32 per hire when a job seeker types the job they are looking for into a search engine.[5]

JOB FAIRS

Most colleges will host a job fair in the fall or spring semesters. Job fairs may be general (open to all majors) or targeted to specific majors. At my college, I host one event specifically for our health-related majors and later, a general job fair, which is open to all majors.

Think of a job fair as a dress rehearsal for a real interview. Dress as if you were attending an interview and bring along several copies of your resume or business cards. When you first arrive, go to the registration table, scan the list of job fair attendees, and select the companies that interest you the most.

Job fair etiquette is unique—you will have only a couple of minutes to talk to each recruiter before being expected to move on to the next table. Use your 30-second marketing statement to introduce yourself. Instead of asking, "What kind of jobs do you have?" use your time to say, "Hi, I'm John Smith and I'm an honors actuarial science major who'll be graduating this May. Last semester I did an internship with Chicago

Metropolitan Health that really got me interested in cost analysis. Would you have any opportunities like that at your company?" After speaking with the recruiter, ask for his or her business card.

In a good economy, employers will be ready to hire on the spot, but more often than not, you will be asked to fill out an application and/or submit a resume. Qualified candidates will then be invited to a formal on-site interview at a later date.

Today, many colleges are offering virtual job or career fairs in lieu of a traditional job fair. The upside is that students can access more employers from a wider geographic distance. At a virtual job fair, students log in to a website during the specific day(s) and time(s) of the event. Participating companies usually provide information about the company and any employment or internship opportunities. Students usually have an opportunity to "live chat" with the "virtual" recruiter, or communicate by phone, fax, or e-mail.

SOCIAL RECRUITING

Currently, LinkedIn and Twitter, and to a lesser degree Facebook, are the most commonly used social media sites for finding a job. In a 2011 survey of students by NACE, 41 percent of students used social media in their job search.[6] Among that group, those with LinkedIn profiles and Twitter accounts were much more likely to use social networking in their job searches than students with just Facebook profiles. Although Facebook dominates the social networking landscape for college students (nearly 91 percent of responding seniors indicated they have a profile), fewer than one-quarter use Facebook as a job-search tool.[7]

For those of you who like to use Twitter, you can find companies and jobs by simply searching by company name. Follow the employers you're interested in and you'll get job leads directly from the companies. Sites like Tweepsearch and Twellow.com will allow you to search company bios, and Tweetmyjobs.com will send you job openings via Twitter.

Google+ is the latest social networking site to appear on the scene. This is Google's latest attempt to create a social network that rivals Facebook, and this time their effort seems to be working. You can create a profile, add your contacts, and even classify them in "circles," which allow you to control what you share with whom. Like Twitter (and unlike Facebook), you can follow anyone you like. This site has a lot of possibilities, especially for job seekers, and will be discussed more in the next chapter.

USING HEADHUNTERS AND RECRUITERS

"Headhunters" concentrate their recruiting efforts in a very specific market niche, e.g., chemical sales, advertising, IT, finance. A company pays a headhunter a fee between 25 percent and 33 percent of the candidate's first year's base salary. Headhunters are most useful for job-seeking students who major in a specific area rather than a general or liberal arts major. To make sure you get on a headhunter's radar, your resume or LinkedIn profile should show "current relevant experience" coupled with significant accomplishments and achievements.[8]

Many industries, from engineering to marketing to health care, use recruiters. Recruiters are employed by a company to fill positions. They are are recruiting professionals, not engineers, nurses, or salespeople, although there are exceptions. For example, some of the nursing recruiters I work with are former nurses.

To maximize the benefit of recruiters you have to understand what their function is and how they operate. A typical recruiter is responsible for filling 15–20 requisitions at any one time. And for each of those openings, they have to work with the hiring manager to develop a position description, then figure out where best to advertise and source for the opening, then post those ads and perform those sourcing activities, and finally, prescreen all of the applicants just to get to the first round of qualified candidates.[9]

Recruiters like to connect with students, so take every opportunity to connect with them. You will have access to recruiters through your campus career center, at job fairs, and at company presentations or other recruiting functions. But remember that hiring managers, not recruiters, typically make the hiring decisions.

The best ways to find recruiters are:

- Google the word *recruiter*.
- Use LinkedIn and search for *recruiter*.
- Use RecruitersDirectory.com.
- Use Wefollow.com, which is a compilation of Twitter users. Search *recruiter*.

COLD-CALLING METHOD

In tough economic times, I often suggest that students contact a company directly, by either e-mail or phone, and inquire about possible job openings. This is called "cold calling" in sales lingo. Another effective method is to ask for a brief, informal meeting to express your interest in the company and learn about any future hiring plans.

Cold calling is often an underused method of finding openings primarily because it involves some legwork (or in this case, telephone/e-mail work) with only about a 10 percent chance of producing results. However, it's that 10 percent chance that can put you in the position of finding an opening that has not yet been advertised. At the very least, you may have a very fruitful discussion with an HR manager who provides you with a referral to another company that *does* have a job opening.

When using the cold-call method, you will experience better results if you have your 30-second self-marketing statement ready beforehand. Begin the conversation by mentioning how you discovered them, tell them why you're calling, and then ask them if they need anyone with your skills (or know of someone who might).

Since 9/11, many large companies will not let you "drop in." Building security will stop you at the door and require that you register at the front desk. You may be able to obtain an application, but probably not be able to speak with someone in HR unless you're very lucky. For these companies, it is more effective to go on their website, search for the HR manager, and send that person an e-mail.

The exceptions to this rule are medical and restaurant industries, small "mom and pop" businesses, and manufacturing plants. These companies are likely to hand you an application and possibly provide an initial interview on the spot. Many hospitality, food services, and retail industries are also open to drop-ins. If you want to apply for a culinary or restaurant management position, pick a time that the business (and the restaurant manager) is unlikely to be busy, such as 10 A.M. as opposed to noon or 7 P.M.

For most professional positions and companies that are likely to have an HR department, you will have to go through their hiring process. Colleges and universities will allow you to drop off a resume but rarely will someone come out and talk to you. These institutions usually have to go through a formal candidate search process. At these institutions, if a new opening comes out, it's better to resubmit your resume, rather than rely on someone to remember to pick yours out of the pile of resumes and include it in the search packet.

NETWORKING

Networking, whether in person or via technology, is increasingly becoming a critical part of an effective job search plan. Not only is networking an effective way to discover job openings, but having a referral for a position can substantially increase the chances of being hired.

Gerry Crispin, cofounder of CareerXRoads, told me,

> Based on my research, when a recruiter looks into their computer system to begin screening candidates they may typically find 100's of resumes—several dozen or more that are fully qualified. In these situations candidates who have networked to uncover an employee willing to refer them are 5–10 times more likely to be presented first, pass the screen, be brought in and hired. It is as if the candidate has moved from a lottery where the chance of winning is 1 in 200 to one that is 1 in 10.

Here's some more sound advice from Gerry:

> The world has changed and we should be demonstrating how 90% of all U.S. jobs can be found in less than 90 seconds. We should help a job seeker calculate from public data the likelihood that a new job will appear in a given . . . targeted firm. We should help them recognize that investing in networking to an employee in a firm with a "published" or "likely-to-be-published" job is more likely to increase their "at bats" than chase unicorns.

THE HIDDEN JOB MARKET

We hear a lot about the "hidden job market," but what exactly does that mean? Let me give you an example. I was talking with an employee of a manufacturing company that supplied electrical products to contractors. This individual had already put an ad in the paper for an electrical salesperson for their front counter and received zero responses to their advertisement. Frustrated, he tried contacting local career centers at colleges offering majors in electronics, electrical engineering, or electrical construction and found the candidates he needed. The next time he needs some sales counter people, he is not going to bother putting an ad in the newspaper—he will go directly to the local colleges (his best source of candidates) and he'll save some money in the process.

There are two things we can learn from this example: (1) as a new graduate looking for employment, you need to identify how and where employers look for candidates; and (2) any future job opening from this company will now be considered part of the hidden job market because they will bypass the traditional classified advertising route.

A common statistic quoted in job search literature is that 75 to 80 percent of today's jobs are not advertised. These unadvertised positions are referred to as the hidden job market. Why aren't all jobs publicly advertised? Primarily because of cost and time. Many employers, in an attempt to keep their advertising costs down, and avoid the flood of unqualified candidates that come with high unemployment, prefer to rely on word-of-mouth referrals or tap into local job pools.

Frankly, the 80 percent figure has always seemed a bit high to me, so I started doing some research but could not find any recent, reliable data to support that figure. Gerry Crispin agrees. He told me that 15–20 years ago, when there wasn't the technology we have today, companies had to rely on advertising in the newspaper. Because it simply wasn't feasible to advertise in every newspaper across the country, there was a lot more hiring by word of mouth (the hidden job market). Today, there are so many more low-cost technological options (websites, job boards) that most companies publish approved openings within 24 hours.

Hiddenjobsapp.com is a weekly blog post about future jobs that haven't been advertised yet, such as those from company announcements of expansion or job creation. When a new company moves into an area or an existing company expands, there is often a media blitz announcing that the company plans to hire a number of positions over a period of time. Technically, these are "hidden" jobs. They are positions that haven't been advertised yet, even though they probably will be in the near future. This equates to a great opportunity for job seekers. By doing a little research and some appropriate follow-up, you could be the first one in the door, before the flood of applications occurs.

From what I have been able to gather, the definition of the hidden job market includes jobs that haven't been advertised publicly: future positions, jobs that are advertised only internally, temporary-to-permanent positions, those filled by word-of-mouth referrals, and those given to staffing agencies to fill. While the hidden job market is certainly a viable source of potential job openings, the number of hidden jobs probably isn't the 80 percent statistic that we were led to believe.

Job openings *do* exist in more places than just in the Sunday classifieds, and many jobs *are* found by networking and won by personal referral. For the best results in your job search, you should use a variety of methods and mediums to source openings: newspaper ads, job boards, company websites, career services listings, social media, networking, and cold calls.

WHERE TO FIND OPENINGS IN YOUR FIELD

In occupations or industries where there are many openings or a short-age of workers, one contact with a recruiter at a job fair is all that's needed to secure a job. Students in highly sought after majors only have to apply to get a job offer. But for other positions job openings may be few and far between, unadvertised, or involve an elaborate screening process. Most people believe that all companies advertise openings and search for candidates in the same way. Much of the advice we hear on the news may be appropriate for business students or those entering a corporate world but not necessarily for students in other majors. To successfully find a job in your particular major, you need to understand how jobs are advertised—what I call the "hiring culture" of that industry or career.

When I speak to dental assisting and hygiene students who are about to graduate, I ask them to take a moment and think about how they are going to find job openings in their field. In other words, where do employers in their career field advertise jobs? Dentists, for example (at least in my part of the country), primarily advertise their job openings by placing an ad in the newspaper or contacting the career services office. Unlike other industries (e.g., engineering firms and IT companies), dentists usually do not list their openings on Monster (although a few large clinics may) and they generally don't attend career fairs. Why? Because the majority of dental offices are small, privately owned practices and the cost of attending a job fair would be prohibitive. So if you were a dental assisting or hygiene graduate and you spent all of your time looking for jobs online at Career-Builder or Monster, you would be missing the majority of the job announcements in your hometown.

The key is to know the "hiring culture" of your industry. Some industries, like the federal government, publicly funded institutions, community colleges, and state-funded colleges and universities, need to be very transparent in their hiring practices and advertise all their openings through a formal search process or bidding procedure. At the college where I work, for example, all faculty and staff positions are advertised in the newspaper. And that's true for most other colleges and universities that receive public funding. However, for other positions, such as those in business, marketing, or sales, word-of-mouth advertising is preferred. The heating, ventilation, and air conditioning, automotive, or restaurant industry may simply put a "help wanted" sign in front of their business. Many of these companies do not have the funds to advertise in the newspaper, or are not equipped to handle the volume of calls they may receive in response to an advertisement. They prefer to have applicants come in and fill out an application—and that's how it's done in their career field. As a new graduate, you will have more success finding openings in your field if you know where and how to look for them.

Some companies, like call centers, often hire large numbers of employees at a time. Because their turnover is relatively high, they rely on recruiters to scour the countryside for applicants and will use all means of advertising necessary. One company that frequently recruits at my college, a nationwide insurance company specializing in handling retirement benefits for customers, advertises positions for their call center in the paper, attends job fairs, and recruits on college campuses. Recruiters for companies like this one also use Facebook, LinkedIn, and Twitter to connect with possible candidates.

WHERE LIBERAL ARTS MAJORS CAN FIND JOBS

Liberal arts graduates, when it comes time to look for a job after graduation, are often in a panic because they think their major hasn't prepared them for anything. This misunderstanding stems from the underlying purpose of their degree. Some degrees, like education, engineering, and architecture, are "professional degrees" and are designed to prepare students for a particular career field such as a teacher, a civil engineer, or an architect. In contrast, a liberal arts or general science degree is designed to provide a body of knowledge (not necessarily get a job). As a result graduates have a broad skill set that can be applied to a variety of positions in the work world.

There are a number of jobs that require a college degree, but not any specific college degree—just the proper combination of skills and experience. Let me give you an example. The following ad was posted on our website and is a good example of a position that does not require any one particular major, although there are several preferred skills:

ABC Skylights, Inc. has a full-time position available for a motivated individual in the Engineering/Project Management department. ABC manufactures heavy-duty, commercial skylights and will be adding new products to our product line later this year.

We are looking for a graduate or about-to-graduate student with strong math and communication skills. Working with customer service is part of project management and the candidate will need to be comfortable helping customers on the phone and in person. The individual will need to be able to travel to job sites to measure and coordinate installation crews. AutoCAD experience will be very useful in this position. It would also be helpful if the candidate has some machine shop experience because project managers coordinate jobs with shop personnel.

Applicants should include his/her field of study and any life experience he/she may have. On-the-job training will be conducted. This is a good opportunity for a graduate who is willing to learn and has a can-do attitude.

Notice that this company was not looking at the student's major (although they would take a technology/engineering student) as much as they were looking for someone with the right *attitude*. Liberal arts and general science majors, with the right attitude and skill set, could successfully compete for this position.

For some jobs, having the right degree or certification is important. For others, having the right skill set is more important than the degree. In a phone interview published on Selloutyoursoul.com, Michael Edmondson, coauthor of *How Liberal Arts Majors Can Succeed in Today's Economy: A Workbook*, suggests that instead of telling an employer what you studied, tell them what skills you acquired in your degree that can help their company. He says,

Shift your thinking from content to skills. Don't sell yourself as a history expert. Just because your problem-solving skills are in analyzing historical data doesn't mean that you can't use those same skills in a market research position. The content of your degree and research projects doesn't matter. It's the skills that are valuable.[10]

In answering the question of what the biggest mistakes are that liberal arts majors make on their resumes and in cover letters, Edmondson replied,

Most people will write, "Ohh I graduated from this college with this degree." That's the absolute worst way to start a conversation with someone. It should be. "Hi, I'm an excellent communicator. I'm very good speaking in front of people. My weakness is that I'm a bit impatient, but I'm aware of that and I'm willing to work with that. But I can offer you my skills as a very good presenter, excellent researcher, and good writer."[11]

Most liberal arts graduates (and graduates in general) do not have enough prior work experience to qualify for positions. That puts them in the common catch-22 position of not being able to get a job that requires experience because they can't get a job to *get* any experience. As a college graduate, you don't have a lot of work experience. But what you do have is plenty of transferrable skills that you obtained through your course work, internships, or research projects—skills such as identifying, analyzing and solving problems, synthesizing complex information into manageable parts, teaching, mentoring, or tutoring, handling quantitative data, working in a group to solve a problem, interacting with people from different cultures, and a whole host of others. All of these skills are applicable to positions in business, local, state, or federal government, or the nonprofit sector. Liberal arts graduates can also look for entry-level openings in large companies (utilities, insurance companies, call centers). Once in the door, there is ample room to move around within the company and even move up to supervisory positions. Other possible positions are working as a recruiter, writer/editor (for those with good writing and editing skills), public relations, sales, customer service, and banking positions such as a loan officer, just to name a few.

HOW TO FIND NONPROFIT JOBS

If you are interested in working in the public sector, a good place to begin your nonprofit search, according to Mary A. Wasmuth, former librarian and job aide, is Idealist.org, http://www.idealist.org.[12] Idealist offers a searchable database of more than 64,000 nonprofit organizations as well as extensive resources for nonprofits. *The NonProfitTimes* publishes an annual list of the 50 Best Nonprofits to Work For, and Opportunity Knocks (http://www.opportunityknocks.org) publishes an annual list of those nonprofits that garnered its Best Nonprofit to Work For awards.

Employer research is just as critical in this sector as it is for the private sector. Targeting organizations, researching, and tracking employment listings on their sites can substantially improve your odds of finding a job that you'll love.

HOW TO FIND GOVERNMENT JOBS

About 2 million people are employed in a government job, making the federal government the United States' largest employer. Only 15 percent of these workers are located in Washington, DC; the rest work in federal government jobs throughout the United States and overseas. Government employees are hired in just about every career field and in a wide variety of occupations. The salaries for most government jobs are based on a "General Schedule" pay scale.

USAJobs.gov is the federal government's official source for federal government job listings, job applications, and employment information. At the state level, your state's civil service website will include openings as well as directions on how to apply. To apply, you must complete a standard resume, describe your relevant knowledge, skills, and abilities, complete any required essays or online questionnaires, plus supply any additional supporting information called for in the vacancy announcement. Many government positions will require a Civil Service Exam. Questions in the Civil Service Exam are generally split between those related to general knowledge and academics, as well as specific knowledge requirements based on the job.

In the government vernacular, *keywords* communicate skills and abilities. When selecting jobs to apply for, study the job description, determine important keywords, and match your skills, experience, education, and knowledge to the job description. Take the time to read the directions and thoroughly familiarize yourself with these concepts. Use the keywords critical to your profession in your resume. The application process is a bit daunting and quite lengthy, but well worth the effort in terms of salary, stability, and benefits.

FOLLOW-UP

Keep a detailed contact log and continue to follow up every two to four weeks until the position is no longer open. Unfortunately, there are many companies today that will only accept applications online. The frustration is that you may never hear back from these companies unless they are interested, and then a call or e-mail asking you to immediately participate in an interview will suddenly appear out of the blue. That's why it's a good idea to keep detailed records of your online applications so you don't forget who you applied to when.

If you are tired of dealing with online "black holes," choose more productive ways to get in front of hiring personnel such as mailing or faxing your resume directly to a hiring manager, or attending industry events, conventions, employer open houses, and job fairs where you can talk to a "real" person. Better yet, use Twitter or LinkedIn to follow and connect with recruiters.

FIVE

The Importance of Social Networking

It's not what you know but who you know that makes the difference.

—Anonymous

Did you know that the number one way people land jobs today is through referral? That's what the annual CareerXroads *Source of Hire Report* survey of Fortune 500 companies found.[1] Their 2011 study showed that, as in years past, the largest number of new hires (external) came from referrals.

As a graduate, your biggest challenge is to find a job. If you can't find job openings through your local paper or online, then how are you going to land a job? The answer is through networking. Talking with someone who talks to someone else, who talks to someone who knows about an opening at their company that would be perfect for you, is networking at its best. Networking is all about reaching out and touching people you don't know and have never met. And you can do this through your career center, your professors, alumni, professional organizations, your friends, your parent's friends, and so on.

NETWORKING BASICS

I suspect that many students hesitate to network because they think that they have to be a super-outgoing, mega-personality type who can remember everyone's name and their personal circumstances. Networking doesn't have to be about being outgoing, bold, or loud. Networking can be done in whatever manner you feel comfortable and can be nothing more than introducing yourself and asking someone to keep your name in mind if they know of anyone who is looking for a job, *period*. Actually, the best networking is conducted casually, when you're talking with people at a meeting who share your interests, at events like a seminar or professional mixer, or at an alumni function. Talk is focused on what you know and do best—your profession.

Social networking, networking done via e-mail or social networking sites like Facebook or LinkedIn, has made the whole networking experience easier because it has removed the social awkwardness often involved in trying to sustain a conversation with a stranger—the "Okay, *now* what do we talk about?" part. Some people will argue that social networking is eliminating our ability to develop interpersonal conversational skills, but that's a discussion for another day. For job seekers who tend to be on the shy side, social networking provides an easier mechanism for conversing with people they don't know—just get online, create a professional profile, post a notice, respond to a post, and before you know it you're networking.

What networking *does* require is initiative—and that's needed by everyone in order to get a job today.

NETWORKING TIPS

People are beginning to realize that a large network doesn't necessarily reap the best results. More often than not, a small, well-selected group of contacts will provide more support and potential career leads in the long run. Targeting your networking to one or two individuals at a professional organization meeting or mixer is more productive than trying to meet everyone.

Make your contact a purposeful connection. If you belong to a group on LinkedIn, or another social media site, post answers to questions and offer to help others out. By being helpful to others, your connections will be more inclined to help you when you need them.

Be very specific in what you want from the people in your network. People are busy, and if someone is not sure how they can help you, they are likely to ignore you. Instead, be very specific when asking for help. Here's an example:

John, I just graduated with my secondary education degree in history. I see that you are employed at Trenton High School. Can you tell me who the head of the history department is? Thanks.

When applying for a job that was referred to you through a networking contact, mention that person's name in your e-mail or cover letter.

Barbara Smith informed me that you might be looking for someone to fill the production assistant position at ABC radio station. Barbara and I worked together on a fund-raising activity for our local YMCA.

And finally, regardless of the outcome of your job search, remember to thank the contact who got you in the door.

USING SOCIAL MEDIA TO FIND JOBS

Social media has taken networking to the next level because of the ability to network with anyone, at any time of day, in any part of the world. Many of you probably already have a Facebook account. Think of all the "friends" you have and all of the friends that your friends have. By leveraging the tools of the social web, you can achieve networking at its finest.

More and more companies are using social media to find employees. The *2011 Jobvite Social Recruiting Survey* found that nearly 9 in 10 U.S. companies will use social media tools to recruit candidates for jobs.[2] This is up from 83 percent in 2010. A 2011 Society for Human Resource Management survey found than more than half of the organizations in their survey stated that they currently use social networking websites when recruiting for potential jobs.[3] This is a significant increase considering that a little over one-third (34%) were using these sites as a recruiting tool in 2008. In this survey, LinkedIn was the most utilized website (95%), followed by Facebook (58%) and Twitter (42%).

Here's something to think about the next time you post a picture on Facebook. Thirty-five percent of employers polled in a 2009 Career-Builder survey stated they did *not* offer jobs to candidates because of content on their social media profiles.[4]

If you currently have a LinkedIn or Twitter account, good for you! Recruiters fully realize the potential of LinkedIn and Twitter and are really beginning to maximize their usage to find potential applicants. Take advantage of it!

YOUR ONLINE BRAND

A personal online brand is nothing more than the image that you are projecting online. Personal branding has continued to gain popularity over the years as a tool to manage one's reputation online, especially though social networking sites. Think of your brand as your personal and professional reputation among coworkers, professors, social networking contacts, recruiters, and other professionals in your field.

William Arruda, personal-branding guru, defines branding as "a unique promise of value." Arruda advises that you build your brand in a way that's authentic to you and align who you are with what you do and how you do it.[5]

Today's recruiters are using Google searches and LinkedIn to source candidates instead of trolling job board databases. Many are even Googling potential candidates or looking them up on LinkedIn before initiating contact. Recruiters will look at what groups a candidate belongs to, what their interests are, the activities they're involved in, and the accomplishments they demonstrate in their profile. Google yourself—you'll be surprised at what comes up. You may see a link to an old newspaper article announcing that art award you won in high school, or find your name listed in your local newspaper for recently making the dean's list.

As more and more employers turn to social media as a way to find candidates, developing a strong, professional online presence will be crucial in making you stand out among all of the other candidates on the Internet. This means that you, as new graduates, must build a strong online presence if you want to be noticed by recruiters.

You can begin developing your brand through a website, a LinkedIn profile, a Twitter presence, or an online resume. Or, upload a YouTube video of yourself giving a presentation or creating a work of art. Give some thought to what you want to be known *for*. Maybe your professional goal is to be known for being an expert in lean manufacturing, or developing a treatment for laminitis, or becoming the next Steven Spielberg or J. K. Rowling. Developing an area of expertise is generally accomplished over a period of time and through several positions of progressively increased responsibility. Your areas of expertise will deepen, broaden, and branch out to other areas as you move through your career.

Developing a brand assumes that you have a clear career focus and an identified area of expertise. If your future goals are not fully developed yet, then select some short-range goals. Maybe a short-term goal is to provide outstanding assistance to the constituents of a congressional office while you ponder a career in politics or law.

These are the components of a good online brand:

- A clear and simple message (what do you want to be known for?)
- Educational background including honors, awards, internships, volunteer work, related work experience, and extracurricular activities

- Professional goals or vision
- A target audience (employers, industries, or clients/customers)
- Examples of personal qualities that you want others to associate with your brand
- Examples of what you can do for or offer an employer
- Examples of your unique strengths, approach, or style or whatever distinguishes you from others

LINKEDIN

LinkedIn was specifically designed to connect people on a professional level. Think of LinkedIn as a professional social network—a professional Facebook. But instead of sharing personal information with friends, LinkedIn is used to ask questions, share information, and network with professionals who share your academic and career interests.

With over 60 million users, LinkedIn has become *the* online place to network and many recruiters are now regarding LinkedIn as the tool of choice for finding candidates. In a *Wall Street Journal* article, Joe Light describes how recruiters have changed their search tactics:

> Many plan to scale back their use of online job boards, which they say generate mostly unqualified leads, and hunt for candidates with a particular expertise on places like LinkedIn Corp.'s professional networking site before they post an opening.[6]

Lavie Margolin, career coach and author of *Lion Cub Job Search: Practical Job Search Assistance for Practical Job Seekers*, identifies 21 common mistakes people make on LinkedIn.[7] One of them is using a headline of "Job Seeker" or "In transition" as opposed to your profile job title (e.g., Accountant). Although you have made it clear what you want (i.e., looking for a job), you are not conveying what you can do for an employer. Whatever message you are trying to establish about yourself on the Internet should be clear, professional, and compelling to everyone who Googles your name or searches for you on LinkedIn.

Here are some guidelines to help you create a quality LinkedIn profile:

- *Photo*: Upload a smiling, high-quality headshot of yourself (no group photos). Make sure you are professionally dressed and that your picture is set against a solid background.

- *Title (headline)*: Your profile headline is the first thing people will read on your profile, so you need to think of it as a marketing tool. Use this as an opportunity to brand yourself. Use descriptive phrases that are keyword-heavy and accurate, not vague, like "Job Seeker." Write something like, "Honors Marketing Graduate Seeking Opportunity in Social Media Marketing." When writing your LinkedIn headline or title, use a simple, concise statement that describes yourself and what you want to do.

Here are some examples of attention-grabbing headlines:

Creative Graphic Arts Graduate Seeking Entry-Level Employment

Honors Marketing Graduate Seeking Opportunity in Social Media Advertising

Recent Communications Grad with Experience Creating Marketing Campaigns for Fortune 500 Companies.

- *Summary*: Your summary should communicate a clear and compelling picture of who you are and what you can do. Make sure your summary and specialties are keyword-rich and include the types of positions you are seeking. Include the key skills and experiences that are relevant to your industry or career field. Areas to focus on include: professional interests, extracurricular activities, community involvement, professional strengths, accomplishments, relevant work experience, course work, projects, and leadership experience.

Here's an example of a LinkedIn summary:

Strong background in promotional writing and editing. Experience as a reporter for a regional newspaper. Public relations and marketing intern with the Red Cross. Utilized print and social media. Editor-in-chief for the Capital Campus newspaper. Interested in career opportunities in advertising, public relations, or other promotion or writing positions.

- *Education*: Include your major(s), minor(s) and concentration(s), if relevant to your professional goals. If your GPA is above 3.5, add it to the Test Scores section. Highlight any academic awards or membership in honor societies in the Honors section.
- *Experience*: This is the place to include clinicals, fieldwork, practica, internships, summer jobs, work study experiences, extracurricular

activities, and volunteer or service learning activities. Make sure to list *all* of your experiences because LinkedIn will use your work history to recommend connections.

- *Publications*: Include any published papers, research articles, creative or technical articles, books, publications, editorials, presentations, or workshops.

- *Certifications*: Include any current licenses or certifications that you hold.

- *Honors and awards*: List any school- or community-related awards or honors that you received. Also include membership in honor societies, Who's Who awards, dean's list, or winning a merit-based academic scholarship.

- *Groups*: Join groups related to your industry and career interests. The logo of each group will show up at the bottom of your profile illustrating your professional identity.

- *Recommendations*: Get recommended by a few people. Try to get at least one recommendation for each position you've held. You can get recommendations from former employers, supervisors, college professors, or academic advisors.

- *Complete your profile*: Try to complete your profile to 100 percent completeness. That means filling in all sections of your profile including recommendations.

- *Update*: Make sure to keep your profile up-to-date with every new job, award, or activity.

For more information about making the most of all of LinkedIn's features, check out http://learn.linkedin.com and the student video series at http://learn.linkedin.com/students.

Other LinkedIn Features

- *Research companies*. LinkedIn also allows you to research companies and connect with people at companies where you want to work. If you do a search under "companies," you will learn a great deal about the types of employers that hire people with your background. You will also see a list of people in your network who are employed there who may be able to open doors for you. Companies can also post job opportunities on their profile. By "following companies" you can stay current with those that interest you. You can find or use your connections at those companies to provide you with insider information or access to the hiring manager.

- *Join "groups."* Participating in groups is one of the best ways to connect and interact with others of similar interests. For example, if you joined a group for your local chamber of commerce, you would have access to positions advertised exclusively for the members of their discussion group.

- *Search for "jobs."* LinkedIn allows you to search for jobs by title, keywords, or company name. You can save your searches, save jobs you have found, and even do a detailed advanced search. LinkedIn will also tell you how you're personally connected to someone at that company. You can then ask them for advice or information to give you an edge in the interview.

- *Share an "update."* You can use your LinkedIn network to help you find job openings by asking your contacts if they would be willing to inform you about possible job openings. Be specific about the type of job you want. When you update your status, it shows up on all your connections' home pages. The more people who see your photo, read your name, and know what type of job you are looking for, the more the word will get out. Remember to regularly update your progress.

Although LinkedIn recommends that you connect only with people that you know, I generally connect with anyone who requests a connection. My rationale is that LinkedIn is more private, and therefore safer, than MySpace or Facebook because it is professionally oriented. By linking with as many people as I can on LinkedIn, I can maximize my networking efforts. Likewise, if your purpose is to find employment, then you'll do a better job of finding a job by reaching out to as many people as you can.

FACEBOOK

Created in 2004, Facebook is now the Internet's most popular social network, with over 750 million users throughout the world. Although Facebook is not really thought of as a "go-to" site for job seekers, this, too, is changing. In October 2011, Facebook launched a new page for job seekers and employers as part of their Social Jobs Partnership, an effort to leverage the utility of social networks in the job market.

Several job-related Facebook apps have appeared on the scene such as BeKnown (Monster) and BranchOut, which lets you import your LinkedIn profile so you can have a professional profile on Facebook. These are two of the latest apps designed to help job seekers integrate with Facebook. No doubt there will be others by the time this book is published.

A word of caution: be careful of recruiters who want to "friend" you—they can gain access to nonwork areas. Joshua Waldman, author of *Job Searching with Social Media for Dummies*, recommends solving this problem by adding them to a "limited access" list that you then customize privacy settings to limit what they can see. Another option is to create a separate, professional Facebook page and give recruiters access to that page.

TWITTER

Job seekers who are active on Twitter can use Twitter to display their resume. All they need to do is upload a copy of their print resume and it will appear as the background on their Twitter page. Think before you Tweet. After the embarrassing Twitter fiasco involving a former congressman, all of us should know never to say or do anything online that you wouldn't want the whole world to know. Twitter can be a great way to get a job and an even greater way to lose one.

GOOGLE+

Google launched its own social networking beta site in June 2011. With Google+ you can create a profile similar to LinkedIn, send "stream" updates, upload photos, perform searches, create "circles" of friends at various privacy levels, and "hang out" with friends using Google's version of a voice and video chat room. Google+ has the potential to offer users the same levels of engagement and interaction as other social networks, along with the benefit of the open network and the ability to share information with a "public" stream (like on Twitter).

NETWORKING TRENDS

According to the 2011 Society for Human Resource Management (SHRM) survey, one-fifth of organizations (20%) do not use social networking sites, but plan to use them in the future.[8] Only 21 percent stated that they currently do not use social networking sites and have no plans to do so in the future.

More and more companies are using Facebook and LinkedIn to verify employee information at two main points in hiring process: (1) before they decide to bring you in for an interview, and (2) after the interview. Employers who conduct their own background search of a candidate by, say, doing a Google search of his or her name may decide not to hire you based on the type of friends you have, their backgrounds, or the types of groups you associate with. It's guilt by association. However, these employers could potentially open themselves up to liability by viewing information that legally cannot be used in the decision-making process. For example, by seeing that the candidate is a certain religion, they open the door to a discrimination suit on the grounds of religion if they don't hire him or her. If, however, they fail to perform a background check, and hire somebody with homicidal tendencies who one day kills his or her coworkers, they may be liable for their failure to have performed due diligence. These are all issues that employers and employees today will have to sort out. The bottom line is this: be very careful about what you post on line. Posting a picture of you dancing on top of the table at a party may seem like a good idea at the time, but remember that whatever you post on the Internet is there for the world to see—and that includes potential employers.

Another trend is the development of *talent communities*, a community of talented prospective candidates. Joining is as easy as becoming a fan of a corporate Facebook page. Candidates in talent communities often feel they are receiving a personal touch. Recruiters interact personally with members of the talent community, and candidates will frequently get e-mails and other messages about jobs and about the status of their own candidacy. They may receive periodic requests to update their personal information and keep their address and e-mail current.

An NACE survey of college students found that job seekers, including college students, still prefer to use social media (primarily Facebook) for communicating with friends and not for finding jobs. However, LinkedIn and Twitter are used more frequently by job seekers to find jobs.[9]

According to a Workplace Coach webinar that I recently attended, HR departments plan to implement broader and more strategic social media outreach. They recognize that social media sites are the way to find top talent—namely, places to post jobs, follow top candidates, and even identify potential candidates in their freshman or sophomore year. The trend in the recruiting world is to develop and build relationships earlier in the student's career—long before they're hired. If you haven't graduated yet, begin connecting with recruiters on LinkedIn and follow them on Twitter. Developing relationships with recruiters early in your college career may lead to a job when you graduate.

Here are some guidelines for safely and successfully using social media:

- Remove inappropriate status updates, Wall posts, and pictures. Whether you like it or not employers are already looking at your profile.

- Use privacy settings to lock down your profile. However, realize that privacy settings can get you only so far—employers can access your profile if they have the right connections and tools.
- Some social media job search experts have recommended using targeted Facebook ads. For example, "Are you looking for a business-savvy IT employee? Hire me!"
- Include employment and education information in your profile. Some people actually have a professional page in addition to their personal page. Think of this as a network within a network.
- Invite connections to "like" your professional page.
- Join groups and pages related to your career. "Like" dream companies, for example.
- Search the Facebook Marketplace. This section has come a long way and jobs are posted there.
- Update your status periodically (but not so often as to be annoying). Be upbeat, and give readers a short update about your employment situation.
- Don't say anything negative—it's a red flag to hiring managers and recruiters. No one wants to hire someone who is negative. Complaining, even if you're justified, may hurt your chances of employment. Don't talk about other companies, employees, past coworkers, or supervisors because you never know who's connected to whom. Assume that an employer can see anything that you write. Remember, the Internet is forever. Anything you do and say, and anything your friends do and say, can be used against you.
- Be careful of what you "like" because this may be used as an endorsement of something that may turn off an employer.
- Don't be inconsistent. Your education and employment information should be the same on Facebook as it is on LinkedIn or Twitter. Inconsistencies will throw up a red flag to potential employers. Know that recruiters will be more vigilant in the future about checking references and authenticating a student's qualifications and identity.

In the 2011 SHRM poll, privately owned for-profit organizations were more likely to use social networking websites, followed by nonprofit and publicly owned for-profit (tied), with government agencies using social media the least.[10] In looking at the types of industries that use social media for recruiting, health care, social assistance, and professional, scientific, and technical services were the big users of social media while the arts, publishing, real estate, biotech, telecommunications, and pharmaceutical industries used social media the least.

While social media can expand your network beyond the local community, this does not mean you should abandon traditional job-searching methods and not participate in area activities and networking events. When job seeking, it is best to divide your time appropriately between social media and traditional methods of job searching.

SIX

What Employers Are Looking for in Your Major

The definition of insanity is doing the same things over and over and expecting different results.

—Unknown

What are employers looking for when they interview candidates in your field? Many job seekers assume that the techniques used to find a job in one major are the same ones that are used to find a job in *every* major. While some employers may rely on similar advertising strategies to announce job openings, other employers may prefer to source, or find, applicants using whatever methods have yielded the best results for them in the past. Local restaurant owners, for example, almost never advertise their job openings on a job board or through LinkedIn. More often than not, they'll advertise through your college's career center, notify your faculty, or place a "help wanted" sign in the window of their restaurant. The trick for job seekers is to know who does what, in which industry.

The expected interview apparel can vary from major to major. If you are applying for a job in a trade or technical field, you probably won't have to wear a suit to the interview. A nice pair of Dockers and a buttoned shirt will be just fine. But if you are interviewing for a finance, engineering, or marketing position, full business professional attire is required (and expected) for both men and women.

Just as job-seeking techniques differ from one major to another, so will the types of questions asked during an interview. Although graduates of any major may be asked some of the "common" interviewing questions usually cited in reference books, the interview will quickly shift to major-specific or technical questions that directly pertain to your career or industry. Teachers will be asked questions regarding their teaching methods, engineering majors will be asked how to solve engineering problems, and accounting majors will be asked about the latest accounting software packages. Examples of some of these major-specific interviewing questions can be found in Appendix C.

The following section includes job-seeking tips, strategies, and advice for job seekers in a variety of majors. Professors and department chairs from universities across the country were asked what skills they felt graduates in their discipline needed to possess to be successful in their profession. Their responses are included in the following.

ARTS

Art

According to a guide by the Fine Arts Career Center at the University of Texas in Austin, fine art is a complex career because the artist is often his or her own employer and promoter:

> Because it may take many years to develop a career as a successful artist, most graduates initially seek ways of earning a living other than from sales of their personal work. It is advisable for art students to prepare for the job market by developing strong computer skills. Knowledge of business as it relates to one's career is helpful for any artist. Artists are creative problem solvers, enjoy experimentation, are self-disciplined, and are visually aware. However, many of the skills learned are transferable to a variety of sectors and jobs. For example, understanding formal elements such as color, line, and space is important for an art teacher, museum curator, display designer, or independent artist.[1]

Graduates in painting, printmaking, weaving, ceramics, photography, sculpture, and drawing should try to find opportunities to exhibit their work and look for calls for submissions in publications, journals, and newsletters as well as receptive restaurant owners, community arts centers, libraries, banks, and other public spaces to show their work.

EMC Research conducted a national survey of employers regarding plans to hire new graduates in the upcoming year. The study was commissioned by the Academy of Art University in California. As part of their survey they asked employers to identify the skills they see as valuable in new college grad job candidates. While computer skills, writing, and analytics are highly desired skills, companies are also seeking new employees with strong technology, creative, and arts abilities.[2]

The top five skills in new college grad job candidates in the creative arts fields are:

- Demonstrated computer proficiency
- Demonstrated analytical skills
- Demonstrated writing ability
- Demonstrated ability and experience using newest technologies
- Demonstrated creative ability

As an alternative to a formal portfolio, consider creating a website to display your work, either online or on YouTube. Sites like http://www.artistportfolio.net can help you create a website to display your photography, paintings, sculpture, and even dance routines. Employers will be very interested to see samples of your work, and giving them an option to view these samples online is a convenient way to set yourself apart from other applicants. Don't forget to highlight any awards that you won, especially if they're relevant to the job you're seeking.

Graphic Design

Graphic design students must be able to adapt to rapid changes in technology according to Bill Karlotski, chairperson of the Commercial Art Department at Luzerne County Community College in Nanticoke, Pennsylvania. In addition, Karlotski says that good interpersonal communication skills and a solid sense of design will give graduates an edge in the marketplace.

Graphic design students should look for openings with advertising, marketing, and public relations firms, manufacturing companies, colleges and universities, and basically any company that sells products online, has a catalogue, or has an advertising or marketing department.

Graphic design students need to pursue leads from a variety of sources. "The ones who work the hardest towards presenting themselves in a professional way are the most successful," says Karlotski. Good advice for students in any major.

Music

The music industry is broad in scope and encompasses education, retail, wholesale, manufacturing, importing, exporting, publishing, performance, recording, repair and rebuilding, tuning, and other businesses. People who are successful in the music industry frequently have training and experience in both music and business. Often the trick to finding a position in the music industry is knowing where to look. George Howard writes, "The problem most people have is that the typical moves one makes to get a job in other industries don't seem to apply to this one. If you want to be a doctor, lawyer, accountant, hair stylist, etc., there is a fairly standard path to take that will lead you to your destination."[3]

Many music careers, such as in the record industry, do not have a clear path. One way to start making those ever-important contacts and gaining knowledge is to intern or volunteer. Experience and word-of-mouth contacts and referrals will be key.

Those who want to work behind the scenes, such as a stage manager, sound technician, mixer, producer, or recording engineer, may find employment with a local or well-known regional band. With experience, they work their way to larger and more well-known bands.

Volunteering, "shadowing" other individuals performing the type of work you want to do, or working for a community, church, or school production will provide valuable experience that will help elevate your marketability in the music business. Being able to work well with all kinds of people and having good organizational skills, a strong sense of responsibility, a good ear for music, and a real passion for music in general are skills that potential employers in the music field are looking for in candidates. Remember that the competition for behind-the scenes positions is very stiff and you may have to take an entry-level job as a "grip" and then work your way up.[4] Trade journals, professional organizations, networking, and hanging around clubs, theaters, concert halls, and other entertainment venues will give you the opportunity to make contacts that may materialize into jobs in the future.

To gain entry as a record producer, getting an internship or externship at a recording studio is a good way to build contacts and experience. Although working at a large recording studio in New York, Los Angeles, or Nashville will offer the best possibilities, there is much to be gained by working at several smaller recording studios as well.

Music education involves a more standardized path, and most graduates apply for these positions in the same way that all education majors do—through their education career centers or directly from school postings.

Composers often write works on commission. Creativity plus being able to work with many different types of people and having diplomacy and negotiation skills are important in this business. Some composers look for grant and competition money to pay for the commissioning of new works. In the more commercial arena, composers may create music for movies, jingles, multimedia projects, video games, or Broadway revues, or they may arrange, adapt, or transcribe the work of other composers. Being able to network and get your name "out there" is critical.

Music therapists use music to accomplish therapeutic aims: the restoration, maintenance, and improvement of mental and physical health. Music therapy positions can be found by applying to hospitals, treatment centers, nursing homes, hospices, rehabilitation centers, and mental health clinics.

Music critics are a unique combination of journalist and musician. Their views are published daily, often providing quotations to be used as publicity for performing artists. More than two-thirds of the music critics in large U.S. cities majored in music, with performance and then music history identified as the leading areas of specialization. Nearly half of the music critics have earned at least a master's degree.

Photography

In today's competitive market, photography students must not only be skilled in their craft, be proficient with the latest equipment and technology, but be able to market themselves and their work.

How do photography students find jobs? With some effort. Photography students must take a proactive role in marketing themselves and look for openings beyond traditional employers. One of my former work study students was a photography major. Photography jobs, at least in our area, are few and far between, so we all had our doubts about whether or not she was going to find a job when she graduated. Then a local online pet supply company called the office looking for a photography student. This company had their own in-house studio and was looking for a photographer who could take pictures of products for several annual catalogues that they produced. Long story short, Lucinda landed the position.

The best part about this story was that Lucinda uncovered an employment source that, until recently, wasn't even considered an option for photography majors. Companies that sell products online (e.g., mail-order companies, after market automobile supply companies, pet suppliers, etc.) will hire photography students and are a good-paying, stable alternatives to traditional photography positions.

Theater/Performing Arts

Most successful actors and actresses have paid their dues by performing in a variety of situations including local, community, and school productions, summer stock, and touring companies. Actors and actresses should be articulate, with clear, pleasant speaking voices. They should be poised and have the ability to perform in front of people.

Individuals working in any field of entertainment need to have a thick skin. They should be able to deal with rejection, which everyone runs into at one time or another in their career.

A stage manager must know at least a little about everything in the theater: acting, directing, set design, lighting, and costuming. The more knowledgeable the stage manager, the more successful she or he will be in the job.

A great combination in a college graduate is a college degree with at least one theater-related internship, additional formal training or study, and experience working in the field (such as working crew on a production, volunteering, teaching drama at a local arts center, etc.). Enthusiasm along with a positive attitude and perseverance will go a long way to sustaining a theater graduate in their career.

BUSINESS

Accounting

According to the Accounting Education Change Commission, to be successful in their careers accounting graduates need skills and abilities that go beyond accounting technical knowledge. These include communication skills, analytical skills, and interpersonal skills.[5] Accounting employers are also looking for evidence of ethics, attention to detail, the ability to process large amounts of data, the ability to work independently, and professional appearance and behavior.

Employers who interview new accounting graduates like to see involvement in major-related clubs and extracurricular activities such as Beta Alpha Psi, the Student Chapter of IMA, the Accounting Club, the Accounting Honor Society, or volunteering to help taxpayers file their taxes through the Volunteer Tax Assistance Program or assist a United Way agency to do its accounting work.

Kathy Adams McIntosh, eHow contributor, recommends these portfolio tips for an accounting clerk job interview:[6]

- The portfolio should include your resume, references, and sample accounting projects from school or internships.

- The organization of the portfolio communicates your ability to remain organized on the job.
- Some job applicants even tailor this organization to mimic an accounting system. For example, each document may be organized according to a chart of accounts. This allows the applicant to demonstrate their understanding of the chart of accounts, along with their organizational ability.

CareersinAccounting.com offers this advice to graduates:

The main skill that will differentiate those who make it to the top is the ability to interact well with people. In a public accounting firm setting business success depends on getting your client to want to do business with you, to want to use other services offered by your firm and to understand the various accounting factors that arise. In a corporate setting, it's even more important to be able to engage with colleagues across the organization and to elicit cooperation.[7]

Where do accounting graduates find jobs? Many are offered jobs as a result of their co-op or internship experiences. Graduates also find openings online, through their career center, at college job fairs, or from employee presentations on campus.

Actuarial Science

According to the Ohio State University's College of Arts and Sciences Career Services, students should list not only their GPA but also any Society of Actuaries/Casualty Actuarial Society exams that have been taken and passed (pending exams can also be included).[8] Aside from GPA, having taken and passed Society of Actuaries/Casualty Actuarial Society exams is the most important qualification for many employers. Other items to include on a resume are any relevant or related course work, accomplishments during internships, and technology and language skills. Technology and language skills are highly marketable to employers in the actuarial field. Be sure to include all software packages you have used for classroom assignments or independent research. Also, describe your level of language skill (e.g., proficient, advanced, fluent) for verbal and written levels.

Business

Business is an incredibly broad field with disciplines that touch every corner of the work world in our increasingly globally connected economy.

Graduates, regardless of what company they work for, will need to have good people skills, be able to handle conflict, be innovative, be able to make sound decisions, and have good time management skills. Business graduates who want to pursue entrepreneurial aspirations must be creative, innovative, and willing to take some risks.

Steven Schroeder, assistant dean of the Business Career Center at the University of Wisconsin School of Business in Madison, believes that business graduates need to have the following skills to successfully find a job in their major after graduation: work independently as well as part of a team; communication; leadership; ability to influence and persuade; a strong work ethic; and ethics, honesty, integrity, problem solving, and analytical ability.

Regarding future skills that graduates will need to be successful in the business world, many of these same skills will continue to be needed in the future. In addition, business professionals will need to be even more technologically advanced in the future.

How do business students find jobs? At the University of Wisconsin–Madison, the majority of business students find jobs through the Business Career Center. Elsewhere, students find employment through networking, social media, and word-of-mouth referrals.

Marketing

Today's marketing professionals must be creative, imaginative, and able to implement social media initiatives. Marketing graduates should be creative and thrive in a team-oriented, deadline-driven environment. According to CollegeGrad.com, advertising and marketing graduates should be able to thrive under pressure, and maintain organizational and communication skills during long hours and overtime.[9] Flexibility with changing schedules and deadlines is also necessary.

Marketing job interview questions are designed to uncover your creativity and your problem-solving abilities. Your answers should include facts, figures, and measurements as well as an awareness of the psychology of marketing.[10] When applying for a marketing position, research the company you are applying for—its current economic climate, its target consumer, and best practices to reach it. You must be thoroughly prepared so that you can easily respond to marketing interview questions with accurate, interesting, and insightful information.

To find positions in marketing use as many sources for finding job openings as you can: niche job boards, career fairs, company websites, social media, and networking. Use your creativity and your connections with people to uncover openings that are a bit off the beaten path.

Medical Reimbursement and Coding

Sheila Malahowski-Davis, health information management coordinator and associate professor at Luzerne County Community College, feels graduates need knowledge of medical terminology, knowledge of anatomy and physiology, excellent basic computer skills, and knowledge of the Health Insurance Portability and Accountability Act. Skills in the future include computerized coding skills, patient accounting, and reimbursement skills.

Most graduates find jobs on the Internet and through their internships.

Sales

Ken Sundheim advises, "Prior to interviewing for sales job, always ask yourself if you would buy the product or service. In sales just as in life, you can't sell something that you don't believe in. Also, never take a sales job if you don't believe in the marketing department (if applicable) or the current marketing structure."[11] Good advice for aspiring sales professionals.

The sales field is essentially all about communication. While being assertive and having a relatively thick skin when it comes to rejection is a good thing, successful sales professionals also need to know how to listen, empathize with, and relate to many different types of people. No one likes a pushy salesperson. The softer approach will actually win more customers in the long run.

The interview is the critical element in getting a sales job (or not getting one). Graduates should be poised, confident, and comfortable in almost any social situation. The ability to build rapport with an interviewer and converse with everyone you meet will be critical in your career. Employers are looking for initiative, good time management skills, and perseverance. It always helps to have some prior sales experience, but if you don't, pull out examples from school that illustrate your leadership, initiative, perseverance, time management, and people skills. These are the traits that employers are looking for in sales candidates.

COMMUNICATIONS

Advertising

Advertising is a field that requires innovation, so advertising graduates should be innovative as well as creative if they want to be a part of an advertising team. It also helps if you are good at creative art, freehand sketching, as well as developing innovative ideas. Successful job candidates should also have an awareness of current events including what is going on in the international arena as well as in the national and local news.

Bring along to the interview a portfolio with writing or design samples. These are crucial if you want a job as a copywriter or graphic designer. Volunteering or interning with an advertising agency is a great way to get valuable work-related experience while you are still in school.

To find positions in advertising, look for job openings through your campus career center, by networking, by connecting with recruiters, and through social media.

Broadcasting

A recruiter in a midsize television market told me that you have to be willing to start at the bottom and work hard for very little pay for several years before you can make it in the radio/television industry. Not everyone becomes the television personality on the 6:00 news, and even some of them, especially in small markets, do not see a huge reward at the end in their paycheck. But it's all about doing what you love, and if you love the exciting pace of a broadcasting environment, whether behind the scenes or in the spotlight, then do what you have to do to be successful.

WetFeet offers this advice to aspiring broadcasting professionals:

Consequently, employers often couldn't care less where you studied or how well you did on your English papers in college. Rather, they want to know how well you can perform under pressure and whether you bring fresh ideas and an ability to think creatively to the table. As in other talent-driven professions, a portfolio of solid work and hard-earned experience usually outweighs formal schooling. Due to the talent-driven nature of the broadcasting industry, landing a job at a larger station in a major metropolitan area without any experience is next to impossible. Rather, most inexperienced job seekers start at smaller stations in rural areas or small towns to get the experience they need to work their way up the ladder. Unpaid internships are an extremely common means of entry.[12]

Getting connections, hands-on experience, and exposure is what it's all about. Graduates should definitely participate in as many internships and co-op experiences as possible. And when that's not possible, volunteer— just to have some experience to put on your resume. Behind-the-scenes camera operators must know their equipment and the technology, be detail oriented, and have a good eye for composition.

Journalism

To be able to get a good job in journalism Andrew Petonak, journalism instructor in broadcast communications at Luzerne County Community College, says graduates need a healthy selection from the following skills: observation, research, and interviewing, writing/copy editing, web and print design, ad design, social media, reporting and feature writing, script writing, photography/video production, and critical thinking skills.

Journalism graduates at Luzerne County Community College typically find jobs through their internships, word of mouth, or instructor recommendations.

In the new age of digital media, the opportunities at newspapers have become limited. Smaller newspapers tend to be more resilient than large newspapers, and online news sites like Patch, Yahoo, and Bloomberg are, for the moment at least, growing and hiring, according to Tony Rogers, an About.com guide.[13]

Volunteering, interning, or freelancing can serve as another way to gain industry experience, while also providing an "in" at certain news organizations. The Internet can also serve as a place to get work published. In some cases, an aspiring writer's work can be noticed by the right person, leading to new opportunities in the field of journalism.

Journalismjobs.com offers the following advice[14]: "While a strong cover letter and resume will get your application noticed, your clips can help you get an interview, and ultimately, a job."

Here are some helpful hints:

- Submit 6 to 10 of your best clips. Include leads with varying styles.
- Your clips should reflect a range of your abilities. For example, they may include an investigative piece, a story you broke, or a human-interest story.
- Select clips that are relevant to the job you're applying for. If you're looking to cover crime, you should include stories that show your resourcefulness and ability to ferret out key details.
- Make sure your clips are dated, well organized, and easy to read. Submit clear photocopies on 8½" × 11" paper. Don't try to impress an employer by putting your clips in a leather-bound case.
- Make sure your clips were written within the past year.

Regarding future skills/knowledge needed in the profession, Petonak predicts, "Writing, reporting, and design will continue to be vital; however, majors will need to incorporate these skills in a more 'blended' digital media environment. Additionally, employers will expect majors to possess a broader skill base as mass media outlets continue to emphasize convergence in delivery, design, and operations."

CRIMINAL JUSTICE

Criminal Justice

With the way our world is today, graduates should have no problem finding positions in the criminal justice field. There will always be a need for investigators, police officers, forensic examiners, and other related criminal justice professionals.

Job candidates may be required to take entrance exams or written, oral, psychological, and physical exams, as well as undergo thorough background checks. Maintaining a clean background is imperative. The minimum age requirement for any criminal justice job is 21. Candidates seeking law enforcement careers must pass a physical examination, which includes tests for vision, strength, agility, and hearing. Law enforcement positions also require passing a written exam and background check, as well as lie detector and drug testing.[15]

According to Timothy Roufa, About.com guide, when agencies consider candidates for promotion, everything matters, including personal appearance. When a department is looking to promote someone, they are looking for the person they feel can best represent the department in every aspect. To move up in the field of criminal justice, listen to the feedback of your supervisors, make changes where needed, and make it a point to develop a reputation as a team player and as someone who can get the job done.[16]

Graduates can find jobs through criminal justice-specific classifieds, job postings, and websites. Check websites of your local and state police, court systems, and prisons. Visit websites of professional associations such as the American Criminal Justice Association, the American Jail Association, and the American Correctional Association, and check trade periodicals such as *Security Magazine* and *American Jails*. Networking with people in the criminal justice field is always helpful especially when looking for jobs in your local area.

Lastly, add a Specialized Training and Skills section to your resume for self-defense training, firearms safety courses, and other certifications.

Forensic Science

Forensic science is all about problem solving. Professionals look at the evidence to see what it's telling them and determine how to use the evidence, scientific tests, experts, and their own knowledge to answer questions and solve problems.

In an interview for AllCriminalJusticeSchools.com, Michael Howard, forensic scientist, was asked what skills are most important to hone:

> You need to understand scientific principles. You need to know how to conduct an experiment, generate a theory, and then see if you can make it fail. In DNA, you have to know enough biology to understand genetics. In firearms testing, you need know physics, math, how things ricochet and how trajectories can be figured out.
>
> You've got to understand the instrument you're using, how a mass spectrometer works, what it's doing, what it's telling you; how you might get a false positive or false negative reading. You have to take notes, write reports, and be articulate enough to explain complicated science to a jury.[17]

Mitchell Holland, PhD, director of the Forensic Science Program, and Jenifer Smith, professor of practice, both at the Pennsylvania State University, believe that forensic science graduates need a strong foundation in the sciences, mathematics, and statistics; strong oral and problem-solving skills; strong writing and documentation skills; and extensive practical and hands-on laboratory-based experience. More than that, they need to be able to *apply* those skills to the field of forensic science as well as have a clear appreciation for ethical principles and behavior.

Communications skills are important and are particularly challenging in forensic science, since the recipients may have little or no scientific training.

How do graduates find jobs in forensic science? Through networking, trade journals, professional meetings and conferences, and social media.

Drs. Holland and Smith predict that in the future, graduates will need professional certification, an understanding and implementation of efficiencies and automation, and a broad international perspective of forensic science.

HEALTH CARE

Dental

Both dental assistants and hygienists need to have outstanding people skills, as well as strong technical skills. A dental hygienist instructor told me that she believed it wasn't so much the skills that dentists are looking for during the interview process as it was the person themself, and how they were "selling" themself through their own individual personality. Dentists want to know if the candidate is going to be compatible with the existing staff members, and if their philosophy is consistent with the current office philosophy. Once candidates can get past this, then employers will look at all the skills that go into being a registered dental hygienist.

The dental assistant has to be able to communicate with patients, maintain confidentiality, be X-ray certified, be competent in chairside skills, know dental materials, and be knowledgeable and competent in all aspects of infection control. It is important that dental assistant graduates participate in continuing education because the field of dentistry is constantly changing.

During the interview process it is not unusual for dental assistants to have a "working interview." This is usually a half-day event where the candidate works alongside another dental assistant and demonstrates his or her skills in a live setting. Usually around lunchtime, the office manager will thank the applicant and let him or her go. Some dental offices may want you to stay all day, so be sure to ask about the length of time beforehand. Some potential employers will pay you for the day; others will not. Either way, you should graciously accept the invitation to do a working interview, if you want the position.

How do dental graduates find jobs? Most employers will advertise in the newspaper or through a college's career center. A few of the larger clinics will advertise on job boards such as Indeed.com and CareerBuilder.com, or a niche job board like DentalPost.net. If you're unable to find a full-time job immediately, take a part-time, per diem, or temporary position. Also, be aware that there are dental staffing agencies such as DentalWorkers .com that may be able to provide employment while you are still looking for that permanent job.

Health Education

Health education majors need to be role models of physical fitness and healthy living as well as be skilled in multiple modes of fitness, recreation, and sport. They must have good communication skills for speaking in front of groups or providing sessions to individuals or small groups of people. A physical education professor told me that the ability to project one's voice also comes in handy. Understanding the psychology of behavioral change and the process of skill acquisition is helpful in helping people achieve healthy living changes or learn new skills. All must be combined with empathy and patience. Basic computer skills are now necessary to incorporate technology into education as well as to perform fitness testing and prescription.

Future directions will include keeping up with the latest medical and scientific data and government reports. The need to have more medical knowledge will be greater as we deal with the fallout of self-neglect in our culture. Diabetes, heart disease, joint deterioration, kidney disease, and more will be, unfortunately, commonly seen issues for a large percentage of our population.

Nursing

Each year we hold a job fair for our health sciences majors. Recently, I casually surveyed nursing recruiters about what they looked for in a candidate. What they told me was that they like to see a good attitude (cheerful, helpful, enthusiastic, shows interest, ask questions) and a professional appearance. All of them expressed displeasure at candidates who had tattoos or piercings, or who did not dress appropriately.

Dana Charles Clark, EdD, RN, at Luzerne County Community College, feels that applicants need to have good presentation skills including physical presence, verbal application of knowledge, listening ability, and organization of thoughts. When interviewing, Dr. Clark suggests, "applicants should be prepared to discuss the facility; ask appropriate questions about the position, nursing theory and practice, staffing plans; and have questions ready to solicit information from the interviewer."

The normal process of applying to our local hospitals was to first fill out an application, whether online or in person. One recruiter told me that resumes were not as important as the application. All of them looked at references. Another recruiter told me that students should not list relatives as a reference. As a normal part of the selection process, applications are screened and candidates are invited in for an interview. Interviews were usually conducted by several people, including the direct supervisor of the department, and then given a tour of the facilities.

Candidates were most often asked situational (behavioral) interview questions because interviewers are trying to gauge candidates' problem-solving abilities and critical thinking skills.

One recruiter told me that students really need to apply as soon as the opening is posted. Her particular hospital receives so many applications that they often stop taking them after five days.

Rebecca Bertram, RN, BSN, MSN, and clinical coordinator at the University of Wisconsin–Madison School of Nursing, feels that nursing graduates should possess leadership qualities, excellent assessment skills, assertiveness, dependability, adaptability, and an ease with technology. On the personal side, a positive attitude and a caring, compassionate, sensitive personality, with a sense of humor, are highly regarded in nursing graduates.

Nursing graduates at Luzerne County Community College often apply for positions in facilities where they have spent their clinical time as a student. Word of mouth from earlier graduates and discussion with faculty are other most cited areas, as well as recruiters and job fairs, especially for those looking to relocate.

At the University of Wisconsin–Madison, students will find positions in typical sources (newspaper, recruiter, social media, job fairs) as well as on websites such as Madisonjobs.com.

The future of nursing looks bright as more care will be needed for an aging baby boomer generation. Nurses in the future will need to be comfortable with totally depending on technology as advances continue to be made, and have even greater autonomy and a systems thinking and planning approach. The skills required 10–20 years from now will include greater emphasis on strategic planning, informatics, budget management, team building, leadership, and management of client care and staff. Dr. Clark predicts that the nurse will become a manager of client care with an emphasis on analyzing and synthesizing data, planning, delegation, and evaluation. Bertram adds, "Total dependability on technology . . . a true paperless system, even greater autonomy, keen organizational skills, systems thinking and planning, and a 'take charge' demeanor."

EDUCATION

According to Julie Underwood, dean of the School of Education at the University of Wisconsin–Madison, the skills that education graduates need to possess to obtain employment as teachers are: written and spoken communication skills, assessment skills, evaluation skills, social skills, intercultural skills, intellectual skills, technological skills, conflict management skills, and classroom management skills.

Teachers must be able to assess the developmental level(s) of the students, their ability levels, and what they already know. Ultimately, teachers must be able to answer the question, "Who are these kids and what are they all about?"

Evaluation skills are also important—not just knowing how to teach a lesson effectively but also how to create opportunities for students to demonstrate what they have learned. Teachers must also assess the effectiveness of their own teaching and ask themselves, "What went well and why? What didn't go well and why?"

Regarding social skills, Dr. Underwood says, "Students respond positively to people who can get along with them and appear to like them. Teachers must be able to participate effectively with others in the school, the community, with parents, and other caretakers." Remember what it was like when you didn't get along with or like your teacher?

In a global world, teachers must have the ability to differentiate instruction to accommodate the diverse needs of students in the classroom, whether English-language learners, dis/abilities, or racial and ethnic diversity. Teachers must be able to create a positive learning environment for each student regardless of his or her background.

At the School of Education at the University of Wisconsin–Madison, personal contacts, the WI Education Career Access Network, Internet listings such as the Department of Public Instruction, and job postings at school districts are the top methods students use to find jobs. Other sources are recruitment fairs, the Education Portfolios & Career Services office, and professional publications.

When asked what skills education graduates will need to have in the future, Dr. Underwood predicted:

Ten to twenty years from now teachers will need to know more about technology and be able to use the same applications as their students. Online courses, technology infused into classroom teaching and even online textbooks are in our near future. Teachers will need to be knowledgeable around data collection issues and making data driven decisions. Moreover, teachers will need to be content area specialists, making sure they are up-to-date on the latest information as our world keeps changing. Science is a prime example of this. Most certainly, teachers will need to be in touch with the cultures of their students. They need to realize they are teaching a cross section of our society— whatever it may be in ten to twenty years. Teachers will need to know more languages, be more culturally relevant, and be more in touch with their own background and how it may influence their teaching style. Ten to twenty years is a long time and although no one can predict what popular culture will be, it is always a good idea for teachers to be responsive to and aware of popular culture and other influences on student lives.

ENGINEERING

Engineering is no longer seen as a solo career, but instead one built upon teamwork and ingenuity.[18] Employers want to know: Is this candidate technically competent? Is this candidate trainable? Will this candidate fit in with the current engineering team? Will they share their ideas and help other teammates, if necessary?

When looking for a position, do not simply rely on the want ads in the scientific journals—although this is definitely a place to begin. If you attend a large or well-known university, recruiters will come to your campus to recruit. They will be ready to hire, so be ready to interview. Attending meetings and conferences is a good way to explore your discipline and to meet other professionals and develop an employment network.

Here is some career advice for graduates in mechanical engineering from the Sloan Cornerstone Center:

Employers prefer people whose practical and teamwork experiences make them "ready to produce."

Apart from work experience, students should consider an elective course in public speaking, or get into student organizations such as an ASME Student Section on campus, where they can practice their presentation and "people" skills. Engineers are expected to present ideas and plans to other engineers, management, bankers, production personnel, and customers. Even great ideas are worthless if they cannot be communicated.[19]

Top-notch technical skills are a must for ChemEs seeking new positions, and specific industry experience is important, say recruiters.[20] But chemical engineers also need strong communication and interpersonal skills—qualities not usually associated with technical engineers. In addition, chemical engineers who seek management roles must understand business operations and what drives their industries. In interviews, candidates should show they can wear several professional hats and have excellent technical, design, and communication skills.

According to Charles Ghilani, professor of engineering at the Penn State Wilkes-Barre Campus, surveying engineering graduates need communication skills, mathematics and physics skills, knowledge on Global Navigation Satellite Systems, knowledge on adjustment of observations with emphasis on least squares, knowledge on data analysis and design of measurement systems, and knowledge on legal aspects of boundary surveying.

When asked where most of his students find jobs, Dr. Ghilani replied, "Students find jobs in this order: summer employment in the field, professional contacts at meetings, Internet searches, simply asking surveying/engineering companies, word of mouth, and placement services."

HOSPITALITY MANAGEMENT

The nonstop growth in the service sector means that there will be enough opportunities for everyone—whether new grad or seasoned employee. Graduates do need to be prepared to start small, especially if they're newcomers to the industry, according to Hcareers.com.[21]

In the hospitality industry, as in many other service-oriented sectors, a candidate's attitude often plays a major role in the hiring manager's decision-making process. Communication, people skills, teamwork, and resourcefulness are other key traits sought by employers in the hospitality industry. You will come into contact with a variety of people, and good team-working skills are essential to the organizational success of the business. Being able to find ways to overcome difficulties or approach situations from a different angle are the sort of qualities employers are looking for in managers.

Kate Clemente, DEd, RD, LDN, at Luzerne County Community College, says graduates need to have hands-on experience, knowledge of the industry, critical thinking ability, problem-solving skills, people skills, analytical abilities, and flexibility. When asked what skills or knowledge graduates will need in the future, Dr. Clemente replied, "Technology, and a second (or third) language."

What should culinary students wear to an interview? Dr. Clemente feels that applicants should wear standard interview attire but have their chef's uniform (clean) with them in case they are asked to demo something or immediately go to work.

Hospitality graduates find openings posted in the newspaper and by word of mouth, through social media, and online. Many graduates are also hired as a result of internships.

"On the hiring side, there's a distinct trend in employers looking for candidates with post-secondary degrees and diplomas in hospitality and foodservice-related disciplines," says Jordan Romoff of Lecours Wolfson, a North American recruiter of hospitality executives, managers, and chefs.[22] Employees today are looking for a better life-work balance, and employers are responding with more flexible work environments. Hotels and resorts are at the forefront of incorporating more environmentally friendly materials in their operations. The hospitality industry is greening, and employees will be expected to go green, too.

INFORMATION TECHNOLOGY

Luis Estrada writes in his blog,

The hiring practices at a number of tech companies are somewhat legendary. The recruiting process at Microsoft, for example, often entails answering a number of extremely challenging technical questions and perhaps a few brain teasers. To work at Google, one often needs to have a minimum GPA threshold from an esteemed University just to get in the door.[23]

If you have the time, and the inclination, Glassdoor.com has over 600 interview questions and reviews by people who applied to Apple. Here are five examples of questions designed to test analytical and computational abilities:

1. Approximately how many garbage men are there in California?
2. Explain Ashby diagrams (or Ashby plots) to me.
3. Find all 25+ errors in POSIX API use in a half-page C program.
4. How do you count the number of 1's in a binary string?
5. Write a routine to determine if a linked list has a cycle.

Joel Spolsky, blogger and software developer, offers this advice to computer science graduates[24]:

1. Learn how to write before graduating.
2. Learn C before graduating.
3. Learn microeconomics before graduating.
4. Don't blow off non-CS classes just because they're boring.
5. Take programming-intensive courses.
6. Stop worrying about all the jobs going to India.
7. No matter what you do, get a good summer internship.

"The difference between a tolerable programmer and a great programmer is not how many programming languages they know, and it's not whether they prefer Python or Java. It's whether they can communicate their ideas," says Spolsky.[25]

Local computer information systems (CIS) recruiters in northeastern Pennsylvania told me that they *will* check a student's Facebook page. Other comments included understanding where your job fits in a business organization and having the latest programming skills (Java, PHP, database query programming). Analytical ability is crucial, so list projects on your resume that reflect your analytical ability. Lastly, candidates should be flexible and open to learning new procedures. One owner of a start-up software company said, "Every company is different; if you come in with an attitude or a preconceived notion of how something should be done, that will eventually get you into trouble."

LIBERAL ARTS

Liberal arts graduates can work in a variety of industries, from retail trade and social assistance, to management and sales, to graphic arts. According to the Occupational Outlook Quarterly, anthropology students, for example, know how to conduct ethnographic interviews and studies—skills that can aid them in marketing work when they analyze customers.[26] English majors usually have editing and writing skills, which are essential for media, public relations, and publishing occupations, and geography majors are well suited to location-based urban planning. These are just a few of the many ways that liberal arts studies apply directly to occupations. (See Appendix B for sample job titles and possible employers for selected liberal arts majors.)

PSYCHOLOGY

Jennifer Hillman, PhD, professor of psychology at the Penn State Berks Campus in Reading, Pennsylvania, believes that psychology graduates must have good communications skills, be able to maintain appropriate boundaries, have good writing skills, work well in groups, have good organizational and time management skills, and have good ethics. "You are dealing with someone's life," she adds.

Most of the professional jobs are gotten after going to graduate school. Graduates in psychology find jobs from successful internships, from the newspaper, and through word of mouth. As for the future, Dr. Hillman says that graduates will continue to need excellent oral and written communication skills and organizational ability, but in addition will need to be able to use technology, possess personal initiative, have creativity, manage stress, be able to analyze information, and be adaptable to change.

RECREATION, PARK, AND TOURISM MANAGEMENT

Garry Chick, professor and department head of recreation, park, and tourism management at the Pennsylvania State University at University Park, says that most graduates have generic management and leadership skills. But what employers seek and need most are candidates with problem identification and problem-solving skills.

Most graduates find positions through their department's internship process. Regarding the skills/knowledge that will be required in his discipline in the future, Dr. Chick believes that problem identification and problem solving will still be the most important skills to have. "These are timeless," he says.

SCIENCE

Animal Science

Daniel M. Schaefer, professor and chair of the Department of Animal Sciences at the University of Wisconsin in Madison, believes that successful graduates should have the following characteristics: defined personal goals; demonstration of achievement of those goals; good oral and written communication; ability to work in a team; demonstration of leadership ability; analytical, problem-solving ability; adaptability; the ability to multitask; and quantitative skills.

How do animal sciences majors typically find job openings? At the University of Wisconsin–Madison, most students find a job as a consequence of an internship. Others find jobs through the Career Services office, at a job fair, or through a professional network developed by the student.

When asked to predict what skills/knowledge will be required in his discipline 10–20 years from now, Dr. Schaefer replied, "An ability to visualize the context in which the company functions and imagine a better 'system,' and multicultural capability to facilitate effectiveness in the global market."

Biology

Biology is a major that can lead to many career paths. In addition to being a teacher or researcher, biology majors go on to become forensic pathologists or criminologists, laboratory technicians, research assistants, conservationists, geneticists, marine biologists, chiropractors, physical therapists, physician assistants, pharmacists, and veterinarians. Biology majors who have artistic abilities can become scientific illustrators, and those with good writing/edition skills can become scientific journal or book editors, or science reporters.

A PhD is usually needed for research and development positions. During your university years it is critical that you get experience working both in the lab and in the field. Summer and weekends jobs in biology will really help give you a strong resume when pursuing a job following graduation. Holders of bachelor's and master's degrees in biology are also qualified for applied research, management, or product development positions. Because competition is stiff for wildlife biologists, an advanced degree may be necessary.

In marine biology, experience is necessary, so volunteer or intern at a zoo, aquarium, marine research site, or wildlife rescue center, or with the U.S. Fish & Wildlife Service to gain valuable experience. It is also recommended that you acquire SCUBA certification, a valid driver's license, and have boat-handling experience.[27]

Chemistry

Dr. David Harwell, assistant director, ACS Department of Career Development and Management at the University of Wisconsin–Madison, understands the importance of preparing chemistry graduates for the changing dynamics of the job market especially in the current societal environment. Dr. Harwell says,

> The chemical sciences provide a firm foundation for professional advancement and their chemistry curriculum emphasizes strong technical competencies, analytical analysis, and research. As the competition for employment increases, there is a greater need for differentiation between job candidates. Students should consider training and experiential opportunities in business and soft skills as a way to broaden their versatility. Leadership, business acumen, and communication skills are all important tools to add to their skill set.

The top three ways that chemistry graduates find jobs are through electronic means such as job boards and company websites, networking, and recruiters. In tough economic times, networking becomes much more important. For bachelor's-level chemists, staffing agencies also play an essential role in employee recruitment for large companies.

"Chemists and chemical professionals tend to be highly specialized in niche subfields," says Dr. Harwell. He continues:

Many chemists are the world's best at what they do. However, as external factors change, they can run the risk of being left behind. It is important to be aware of changing demands driven by technological advances and market demands. Continuous professional development, flexibility and adaptability are the keys to career progression and success. The best thing about chemistry is that it favors inquisitive minds, so students can continue nurturing their natural tendency to learn more about our beautiful chemical world.

If you have completed any significant research projects in science courses, it is definitely smart to add a Research section to your resume. Employers want to know that you are able to create, conduct, and analyze experiments or theories and present your ideas in a poster presentation, abstract, or full research paper. List the project name, course title, and the month/year of completion, and then provide a few bullet point descriptions about the hypothesis, thesis, the process, and the results, if possible.

Veterinary Technician

Today's new veterinary technology graduates need to communicate effectively and be professional, says Rosemary Cook, CVT, PhD, Sciences Division chairperson at Johnson College in Scranton, Pennsylvania. Attributes that she believes will make graduates stand out are communications skills and professional behavior such as dressing properly and being on time, a respectful and humble attitude, and a willingness to learn and address challenges.

Dr. Cook says that veterinary technician specialties are on the rise. Graduates can specialize in internal medicine, dentistry, behavior, anesthesia, and critical care to name a few. Diagnostic imaging (digital radiography, dental radiography, ultrasonography, endoscopy, and magnetic resonance imaging) are becoming more popular today and will be in the future. I can personally attest to the growing popularity of diagnostic imaging in veterinary medicine. When my 10-year-old Maine Coon cat began having intestinal problems, my local vet took referred him to a nearby specialty clinic for an ultrasound.

SEVEN

A Word about Professionalism

Professionalism: It's *not* the job you *do*; it's *how* you *do* the job.

—Anonymous

What exactly does professionalism mean? Is it good manners? A fancy title? Dressing in an expensive Armani suit and silk tie? Sometimes.

Professionalism may be hard to describe but one thing is certain—you know it when you see it. Studies have shown that a well-dressed appearance tends to convey a higher level of knowledge and a sincere interest in advancement; on the other hand, a disheveled worker gives the impression of being a disinterested, marginal performer.[1] Your first impression should be a positive message that communicates your confidence and ability as a professional in your field.

The Center for Professional Excellence at York College of Pennsylvania commissioned a national survey on the state of professionalism among recent graduates from U.S. colleges. They found that 38.2 percent of respondents felt that fewer than half of all new graduates exhibited professionalism in the workplace.[2] How do employers judge professionalism? By examining communication skills, judging attitude or demeanor, and evaluating appearance.

Overwhelmingly, 96.3 percent of the respondents, HR managers and business leaders, continue to say that professionalism *does* factor into the decision to hire or not hire an individual. The "ability to communicate" factored as the top method of evaluating professionalism.[3]

Interestingly, the vast majority of respondents (88.1%) thought of professionalism as being related to the person rather than the position. In other words, anyone in any position has the potential to exhibit professional traits. Business leaders (17.6%) were more likely than HR professionals (10.5%) to associate professionalism with positions rather than the person.[4]

The most frequently cited traits or behaviors associated with professionalism were:

- Personal interaction skills, including courtesy and respect (48.0%)
- The ability to communicate, which includes listening skills (46.9%)
- A work ethic, which includes being motivated and working on a task until it is completed (35.4%)
- Appearance (34.2%)
- Self-confidence and self-awareness (20.1%)

The most frequently cited unprofessional traits or behaviors were:

- Appearance, which includes attire, tattoos, and piercings (39.1%)
- Poor communication skills including poor grammar (38.9%)
- Poor work ethic (37.0%)
- Poor attitude (28.3%)
- Being disrespectful and inconsiderate (27.4%)
- Having a sense of entitlement (16.6%)[5]

Entitlement, defined as expecting rewards without putting in the work or effort to merit the rewards, was the most cited reason (21.5%) for a decline in professionalism over the past five years. Employers also reported seeing a spike in text messaging at inappropriate times.

Respondents rated a list of qualities according to how important each is when considering a recent college graduate for a position requiring professionalism. These are:

- Accepts personal responsibility for decisions and actions
- Is competent in both verbal and written communication
- Projects a professional image; is able to think independently
- Demonstrates a passion for one's work; is able to act independently; is able to be flexible

- Has a clear sense of direction and purpose; exhibits loyalty to the company; is able to critically evaluate data
- Does the job without regard for how long it takes
- Has a sense of responsibility to the greater community; tries to maintain a balance between work life and personal life
- Is able to do work that is creative
- Is concerned about opportunities for advancement
- Is an expert in one's field[6]

Professional majors such as nursing, medicine, veterinary science, psychology, and business, among others, routinely stress personal integrity and ethics in their professions. First-year pharmacy students, for example, are usually asked to take a verbal pledge of professionalism, which, among other things, promises loyalty and duty to the pharmacy profession.

Most students begin to get their first real taste of professionalism and form their own professional self-image by participating in professional student chapters. Networking with alumni and interacting with professionals at conferences or career fairs are additional avenues designed to prepare you for professionalism. Your junior and senior classes, labs, clinicals, field experiences, and internships are all professional learning environments where you learn how to conduct business in a professional and ethical manner, treat customers with courtesy and respect, keep your cool in the midst of chaos, deal with a crisis, or defuse irate customers or clients.

Maintaining your demeanor, a hallmark of professionalism, is the one thing that you can control when it seems that your world is completely out of control. Blowing up at someone in the office is never an option, no matter what your major is.

FIRST IMPRESSIONS

How many of you have formed a mental image of what someone looks like just from the sound of their voice on the telephone only to find out they looked entirely different when you met them in person? Think about all the times you formed quick, almost unconscious, opinions about someone's competence, character, intelligence, or commitment after being introduced to them for the first time. Most of these first impressions are formed on the basis of another's appearance, behavior, and communication.

I often tell students that in the absence of available information, it is simply human nature to form your own conclusions. In the job search process, people will begin to create an impression of you from the very first moment they have contact with you—even before you've been invited in for an interview. So remember, whenever you have contact with an employer—whether inquiring about a job, filling out an application, or scheduling an interview—employers are creating an impression of you as a potential employee.

Because of the risk of making a negative first impression, I advise students to cover tattoos by wearing long sleeves and not to wear facial piercings to the interview. Generally speaking, the business workplace is a fairly conservative environment governed by certain rules of dress and behavior. Unless you're planning to star in the next motorcycle chop shop reality show, tattoos and piercings are usually not a part of a professional picture. Finding out about a company's dress code is imperative because it's likely that you'll have to continue to cover your tattoos on the job.

PROFESSIONALISM DURING THE JOB SEARCH

Students who are not able to make the transition from college student to professional are at a huge disadvantage when it comes to competing for a job because companies have the luxury of taking only the strongest, most professional candidates. In the interview, how you conduct yourself is crucial to being hired. Not dressing or behaving appropriately can really make you stand out—and not in a good way.

Body language is also an important part of the professional image. An interviewee who slouches in his or her chair may be interpreted as lacking enthusiasm for the position. Lack of eye contact can be perceived as shyness or lack of trustfulness, and nervous behaviors may signal a lack of confidence. In contrast, a straight posture reflects confidence and attention to detail.[7] Posture and body language influence others' perception of competence.[8] For example, folded arms held tightly against the body reflects a closed personality.[9] This posture may indicate that the person is introverted, lacks confidence, or is nervous; whereas an open posture with arms spread in a relaxed position may indicate the interviewee is confident and willing to engage in the challenges of the work environment.[10] Attention to body language is crucial because negative body language can unknowingly sabotage your interviewing efforts. Therefore it's important to recognize what kind of image you are projecting. Ask your friends, coworkers, supervisors, advisors, and professors for an honest assessment of your professional demeanor.

Technology has allowed us to transcend geographic distance. The downside to all of this technology is that if used unprofessionally, it just gives a hiring manager one more reason to eliminate you from the candidacy pool. When interacting with hiring managers, make sure that your e-mail address or voice-mail message is "grandmother approved."

The following is a simple example of a professional voice-mail message:

> You have reached the voice mail of Justin Jones. At the tone, please leave your name, number, and a brief message. I will return your call as soon as possible.

When interviewing, be smart with your smartphone: turn it off. Loudly chatting on the phone or listening to your iPod as you wait for the interviewer is inconsiderate. While it should go without saying, never respond to a call or text message during the actual interview. And don't text a hiring manager after the meeting—pick up the phone or send an e-mail if you haven't heard back within a couple of weeks.

When applying for positions or waiting for the results of an interview, make sure you provide the interviewer with a cell phone number or e-mail that you check several times a day. Hiring managers won't wait forever, and they generally won't try to reach you more than a couple of times.

I remember a conversation I recently had with a local employer who interviewed one of our students for a restaurant management position. After interviewing the student, they were very impressed with the individual—she was professional and knowledgeable. But when they tried to contact her to offer her the position, she never returned the call. After leaving several voice-mail messages they gave up and hired someone else. Not only did this person lose out on a wonderful job opportunity, but she also "burned some bridges" by leaving a bad impression with that employer. And what many people don't realize is that employers *do* talk with one another. Don't think it doesn't happen.

If you interview for a position that you are no longer interested in, that's fine, but be professionally considerate and let the employer know that you're no longer interested or that you've accepted another position. Don't just leave them hanging.

With all the popularity of social media sites, employers are beginning to check up on potential hires through their Facebook and LinkedIn pages. Unfortunately, most of the time an unprofessional posting or picture will have a negative effect on your job search plans. The other negative consequence of posting photos on social media sites is that photos can result in potential stereotyping based on the color of skin, appearance, dress, situations, or choice of hobbies. This is exactly why you're advised to *never* include a picture of yourself with a resume. Some job seekers create a separate, "professional" social networking page just for the purposes of finding a job.

Watch out for any personal information or postings (by you or your friends) that can damage your reputation or your "hireability." Think about what you post before you post it! "Hide" or delete undesirable posts or updates you receive from others. Employers can potentially prescreen you out of candidacy for alcohol or drug abuse, poor work skills, poor writing or communication skills, politics, ethnicity, religion, disability, gender, or sexual preference. According to an article on the website of *Colorado Biz* magazine, one should also be careful with political commentary, highlighting hobbies that may be considered too risky, or certain types of organizations or groups that you belong to.

Here are some tips to create a positive and professional first impression:

During the interview:
- Be prompt and professional.
- Smile and be gracious and friendly to everyone you meet.
- When a hand is extended, smile and shake hands firmly.
- Enunciate and avoid using slang or unprofessional speech.
- Do not chew gum or smoke.
- Do not become unduly familiar or inappropriately relay private or personal information other than casual comments about extracurricular activities, hobbies, and interests. Remember to keep everything you say or do focused on work.

During a meal:
- Select a meal that is easy to eat since you may be talking more than the other guests at the table.
- After the meal, thank the host.
- As a rule of thumb, silverware selections progress from outside toward the plate.
- Salad and bread plates are placed to your left (above the fork), and drinks are placed to the right (above the knife and spoon).
- During a meal, retain your professional demeanor. Even if it seems to be a more relaxed setting, employers are still forming opinions about you.
- Keep your conversation professional and retain good grammar and articulation. During comfortable interactions, it is easy to reveal information that may not contribute positively to your candidacy.

The overnight stay:
- If you are unclear as to whether an employer will support the costs of your visit or an overnight stay, it is appropriate to ask in advance of your visit.

- If amenities, like room service or snacks, are included, be professional and deal with the employer's resources as if they were your own.
- It is courteous to thank the host for the night's stay and any other amenities offered.

Using e-mail:
- Avoid slang, abbreviations, texting shorthand, and unprofessional signatures.
- Always proofread and spell-check! Nothing creates a negative impression faster than poor grammar or typos in your e-mails.
- Send the e-mail to yourself first to be sure you haven't missed anything. According to Max Messmer, chairman and CEO of Robert Half International and author of *Job Hunting for Dummies*, the rules of writing still apply to e-mail.[11] Hot job prospects can cool quickly if your message is littered with typos or texting shorthand.

Accepting job offers:
- If offered a position, do not keep the employer waiting. Accept (or decline) immediately. If you need more time to consider the offer, ask for it.
- In some situations a verbal agreement is considered as good as signing a contract so don't accept an offer without careful consideration.
- Do *not* accept an offer if you are not sure you want the position. Ask the employer more questions or ask for more time.
- When you accept or decline an offer, do so in writing and be professional in your communication style.
- When you accept or decline an offer, do so in writing and be professional in your communication style.
- When you accept an offer, notify all other employers with which you had interviewed and withdraw any outstanding applications.
- If you face circumstances that force you to renege on an acceptance (e.g., critically ill parent, marriage), you should notify your employer immediately and withdraw the acceptance. If you have accepted a signing bonus, you should return it.

Why does professionalism matter to employers? Because to outsiders, *you* represent the company. Keep that in mind when interacting with clients. What you say, do, or wear reflects on your employer. If you don't demonstrate pride in your work or respect for your company, no one else will.

Although our society has become much less formal in recent years, many employers still desire a certain level of professionalism. If you want to get a good job (or a raise), it is vital that you learn how to conduct yourself in a professional manner and interact with others in a manner appropriate to the workplace or in your profession.

Dr. George W. Waldner, president of York College of Pennsylvania, said it best in a FoxNews.com article: "To land a job in this economy you'll need to suit up, show up on time, and do yourself a favor by turning off your cell phone."[12]

PROFESSIONAL ORGANIZATIONS

Almost every job field has a professional organization. These groups can play a key role in your professional development and keep you up-to-date about what's happening in your industry. Professional organizations often regulate professional standards, promote the interests of their members, and provide a network of contacts that can help you find jobs and move your career forward. Professional organizations and associations provide a wide range of resources for navigating your career. They can offer a variety of services including job referral services, conferences, continuing education courses, insurance, travel benefits, periodicals, and meeting and conference opportunities. Many professional organizations have active student chapters on college campuses. If you're still in school, check with your advisor or major professor about joining one.

PROFESSIONAL IDENTITY

Professional identity is the set of attributes, beliefs, values, motives, and experiences by which individuals define themselves in their professional lives. Although you may not be aware of it, you have been formulating your professional identity since your first contact with a member of your profession. From that person's behavior, you began forming impressions of how a professional in your field behaves and operates.

In your major courses you formalized your theoretical viewpoint, and discussed the concepts of responsibility, confidentiality, conflict of interest, risk and safety, relationships with others, loyalty, whistle-blowing, codes of ethics, professional standards, and licensing. You also learned that professional responsibility can result in liability.

When you begin to practice as an engineer, nurse, teacher, accountant, or other professional role, your theoretical construct, values, and ethics will be tested. As you encounter ambiguous situations, your professional definition will stretch and grow. What importance will you personally place on honesty and integrity, technical competence, or stewardship? Professional organizations can help you develop, strengthen, and maintain your professional identity. So can finding a good mentor or supervisor.

The completion of your degree marks the first formal step in your transition from student to professional. Whether or not you feel like a professional, the fact of the matter is that you are a professional. At the end of the day, professionalism is all about taking pride in being a member of your profession—whether nurse, engineer, or educator. And pride in your degree, and the profession it represents, shows.

EIGHT

Be Prepared for the Interview

A prudent person foresees the difficulties ahead and prepares for them;
the simpleton goes blindly on and suffers the consequences.

—Book of Proverbs

When do you think the interview begins? When I ask this question in class someone usually responds, "When I meet the interviewer."

Actually, the interview begins with your initial contact with a company. That includes the initial telephone call to set up the interview appointment, an e-mail inquiry, when you are sitting in the waiting room waiting for an appointment, or when you are interacting with the secretary or receptionist. With each contact you make with a potential employer, you are providing information that they will use to form an opinion about you—even before you meet face-to-face! Therefore you need to be at your best whenever you have any contact with the employer.

PREPARE FOR THE INTERVIEW

The difference between candidates who ace their interview and those who do not is their level of preparation. Would you go into a final exam unprepared? (Okay, well maybe some of you would.) But if you did, the outcome would probably not be very good. You would have more success and feel more confident if you came well prepared. The same principles apply to the interview.

Being prepared for an interview means that you have done your research on the company and the position, you know what kind of interview questions to expect, and you have an established repertoire of responses (see Appendix C for sample interview questions for specific majors). Take the time to review the "standard" interview questions you will most likely be asked. See "Job Interview Questions and Best Answers" by Alison Doyle at About.com, JobInterviewQuestions.org, or the Job Interview Questions Database at Quintessential Careers (http://www.quintcareers.com).

Sample Traditional Interview Questions for College Graduates

1. Can you tell me a little about yourself?
2. What do you know about our company and why do you want to work for us?
3. How would you describe your ideal working environment?
4. What are your strengths? Weaknesses?
5. How would someone who knows you well describe you?
6. Describe a challenging situation that you have faced during your college years, and how you resolved it.
7. Why did you choose this college?
8. What was your favorite course? Your least favorite?
9. Are you willing to travel/relocate?
10. Why should I hire you?

The more prepared you are for an interview, the more confident you will feel and the better you will perform. I have served on many search committees and I can tell you that good candidates are easy to spot because they really stand out during an interview. So many candidates come unprepared for questions, are not dressed professionally, or project a sloppy, unfocused, or unprofessional image.

DO YOUR RESEARCH

So how do you begin to prepare for your upcoming interview? The first step is to gather as much information about the company as you can. Background information on the company will allow you to respond thoughtfully and intelligently to questions like, "Why do you want to work here?" Researching the company's financial status, clientele, and other facts before the interview will enable you to intelligently contribute to the conversation and ask the pertinent questions to help you make an informed decision about whether or not to accept the position.

Company information, reviews, and ratings are available for just about every major company and many smaller employers. Websites such as Hoovers.com and WetFeet.com provide basic company information. Sites such as Vault.com, Glassdoor.com, Telonu.com, and others provide insider company information from actual employees. Site visitors can read about the company, what it is like to work there, and even get sample interview questions that have actually been asked by hiring managers. Keep in mind that the company reviews on all of these sites are posted by individuals, including those who may be disgruntled employees.

Another method is to Google the company and read company reviews to get the inside scoop from employees and former employees. Search YouTube for company-produced videos with information on employment opportunities and company culture. Use your connections on LinkedIn to find people who currently work or previously worked at the company you're researching. Ask them what they can tell you about the company and what it was or is like to work for the company. This "insider" information is invaluable!

Finally, here's a great tip from Lindsey Pollack, author of *Getting from College to Career: 90 Things to Do before You Join the Real World*: "Before your job interview, study the LinkedIn profiles, Twitter feeds, and blogs of the people you'll be meeting. The more preparation you do, the more confident you'll feel—and the more likely you'll be to make a great impression and land the job!"[1]

DEALING WITH INTERVIEW JITTERS

Everyone experiences some degree of nervousness before, or during, an interview. Even seasoned interviewees still get sweaty palms and a knot in the pit of their stomach, especially if they're interviewing for a job that they really want. A little bit of nervousness can give you the adrenaline edge you need, but too much can backfire and cloud your thinking.

Try to get a good night's sleep before the interview and eat something light before you leave to avoid a blood sugar drop during the interview. And go easy on the caffeine—you don't need to be amped up any more than you already are. Plan to arrive to the interview at least 10 minutes early. By leaving early, you will give yourself the needed time to deal with any unexpected delays, such as getting behind a school bus, or having trouble finding a parking spot. Once you get to the interview location, take a few minutes to relax or head for the restroom and double-check your appearance. Then sit down and concentrate on the task at hand and prepare yourself mentally. If your heart is racing and your palms are sweaty, calm yourself down by taking a couple of slow, deep, diaphragmatic breaths or picture a peaceful scene. Banish any kind of negative self-talk. Instead, tell yourself that you *will* be successful.

TYPES OF INTERVIEWS

There are several types of interviews that you may be expected to participate in.

The Telephone Interview

Many employers will use a telephone interview to initially screen potential candidates. Telephone interviews are generally shorter in length than traditional face-to-face interviews and are designed to narrow the applicant pool to a small, manageable number of applicants who can be invited in for a live interview.

What makes telephone interviews so difficult is that you can't see the person who is talking to you. You can't see their facial expressions and body language—all of the nonverbal cues that people use to determine what people are really saying and how they're reacting to you. Telephone interviewing generally takes some getting used to. The process will be a little easier if you make sure to get the first name of the person who will be interviewing you (write it down if you have to) and try to form a mental picture of that person. When you speak to the interviewer, bring up that mental image and pretend that they're standing right in front of you. Most people find that this technique helps them relax and focus on the conversation.

The following tips will help you perform your best during a telephone interview:

- Conduct the telephone call in a room that is quiet, has good lighting, and is free of background noise like barking dogs or children playing.
- If you are using a cell phone, make sure you have a strong cell signal, or use a landline phone to avoid dropped calls. If for some reason you are in the car when a recruiter calls, pull over to the side and park so you can devote your full attention to the conversation and not run the risk of having your cell phone cut out.
- Lay out a copy of your resume, notes, or a list of "talking points" on a table or counter in front of you (but don't rattle the pages during the interview). If you are asked questions about your background, you'll find it much easier to give quick and accurate responses if you have your resume or notes right in front of you.

- Stand up while you speak on the phone. This will not only help you feel more in control of the situation but allow for good diaphragmatic breathing, which will help you remain calm and give your voice a deeper, fuller sound.

- Smile when you speak and use a pleasant, professional voice. Believe it or not, your facial expressions carry over into your voice.

- If possible, wear a headset. This will allow you to move around and make the normal hand gestures that you would when speaking in person. The energy you create by these movements will make you sound more alert.

- Keep your answers clear, concise, and positive. Take a moment to collect your thoughts and think about what you are going to say in response to a question. Avoid the temptation to rush.

- Recognize that the interviewer is probably taking notes so remember to briefly pause between thoughts.

- Make sure you answer the question that is asked. Do not waste valuable time by rambling, elaborating, or getting off track and telling stories. Provide examples, but keep your illustrations brief and to the point.

Video, Online, or Virtual Interview

To decrease the costs associated with travel, many employers are conducting interviews via distance technology, Skype, or commercial products like InterviewStream.com.

You may want to check with your campus career center to see if they have a subscription to a commercial interviewing program. These programs allow students to record themselves answering interview questions via a webcam, which can then be replayed for self-evaluation.

Video interviewing takes some getting used to, so make sure you're familiar with the technology beforehand so you will more comfortable during the interview. The biggest difference between video interviewing and live interviewing is that your movements are limited to the view of the video camera or webcam. Before a video meeting, do a trial run with a friend to make sure your webcam and microphone are working properly. Make sure you are seated in the center of the video screen, adjust any lighting issues, and remove any background items that may potentially create a distraction while you are speaking. If you are interviewing via a webcam, move your computer to a quiet location and sit against a plain wall or background.

It's generally a good idea to practice recording yourself prior to the interview. Play the recording back and review your performance. Watch for excessive hand gestures, body movements, and vocal fillers like "um" or "like"—all of which will appear to be magnified during the video interview. Dress as professionally as you would in any other interview setting, smile, speak into the camera, and remember to articulate.

The Campus Interview

This is a relatively structured setting consisting of a formal interview with a company representative. Normally you will be asked to register for an interview time with your career services office and turn in a resume prior to the interview. You may have several interviews scheduled in one day, depending on the size of your institution. After the campus interview, you may be asked to come in for an on-site interview. This is the second impression. The on-site interview may involve a number of interviewers over several hours such as an HR representative, your potential supervisor, potential coworkers, and other members of your prospective department. The questions will be much more in-depth and will test your knowledge of the industry, the company, and your own abilities. You also might tour the facility, shadow a staff member, or have the chance to talk more casually with interviewers during the day. Don't let your guard down; these informal chats can be just as important as more formal conversations. Depending on the company, your day may also include a social gathering, such as lunch or dinner. You're going to have to be "on" for quite some time and impress a number of different personalities, so make sure to arrive well rested and prepared.

The Panel or Group Interview

This type of interview consists of being interviewed by several people at one time. Many people find this type of interview structure a bit intimidating until they've gone through it at least once. Typically, you (the candidate) will be asked to sit across from, or in front of, several people. One person may ask all of the interview questions, or each member of the search committee will ask a question. When responding to a question, begin by directing your answer to the person who asked the question and then make eye contact with the other members of the panel while you are answering the question. At the conclusion of your response, direct your attention back to the person who initially asked the question.

The Lunch or Dinner Interview

Some companies will interview students over lunch or dinner or host a reception or buffet luncheon or dinner. Interviewing over a meal is difficult because not only do you have to be on top of your game verbally, but you also have to watch your table manners. Always order something that will allow you to converse naturally, and avoid entrees that could potentially spill on your clothes, like soup, tacos, or spaghetti.

I once hosted a meet-and-greet buffet-style dinner for an automotive company looking for salespeople/customer service reps. The CEO welcomed the group, and the director of HR gave a brief presentation about the company. Everyone was then asked to get something to eat and sit down at one of the tables set up in the room. Several staff people, including the CEO, were interspersed at each table and conversed with students during the evening.

This company was looking for people who had an automotive background, but they were also looking for individuals with certain personality traits that, in their experience, were indicative of good customer service reps. Those they ended up hiring spoke up, asked questions, were passionate about the automotive field, were able to articulate clearly, and conducted themselves professionally (proper dress, proper table etiquette, friendly, good communication skills, etc.). Later the HR director told me that they were looking for students who demonstrated that "something more" quality—in other words, students who showed initiative and interest, and would go above and beyond to produce.

PERSONALITY AND BASIC SKILLS TESTING

Many employers are now relying on objective measures such as personality tests, skills tests, or other instruments to better help them select the right candidate for the job. Some assessments are aptitude tests that test basic math, English comprehension, or communication skills. Others are intended to measure honesty or an individual's values, and still others are designed to gage personality.

Skills and aptitude tests are a common form of preemployment testing. These assessments determine whether a candidate has a specific set of skills required to be successful in a position. These tests can be written or oral and may assess writing, math, verbal communication, and reasoning ability.

Job knowledge tests focus on the professional or technical expertise required for a specific position. Unlike aptitude or cognitive tests, job knowledge tests evaluate what the candidate knows at the time the test is given. These tests often use multiple-choice or essay questions. Basic accounting principles, computer programming, and contract law are examples of subjects a job knowledge test might measure. At my college, it is common practice for a dentist to ask a potential dental assisting candidate to do a "working interview" where the candidate actually works in the dental office for a couple of hours (sometimes receiving pay, and sometimes not) while the dentist evaluates the candidate's dental assisting skills. Some of the call centers in our area ask their candidates to show how they would answer a mock customer service phone call.

Personality tests have been around for a long time. When I worked for a group of psychologists, two of the clinicians provided consultation services to local businesses, namely, administering and interpreting personality tests to potential applicants as part of the employer's interviewing process. Some of the most common traits assessed included extroversion, emotional stability, agreeableness, conscientiousness, and openness to experience. Personality tests have no "right" or "wrong" answers. The questions are simply designed to reveal the candidate's personality traits, and that information can then be used when evaluating the candidate's fit within the organization.

Today, about one-third of employers use testing for hiring and promotions, according to a recent MSNBC.com article. In the article, Josh Bersin, president and CEO of Bersin & Associates, an Oakland, California, research firm, was quoted as saying that he estimates that this kind of pre-hire testing has been growing by as much as 20 percent annually in the past few years, driven in part by high unemployment.[2] Industries that are flooded with resumes such as retail, food service, and hospitality are among the ones that use these tests most often.

Personality tests can be useful when used appropriately and interpreted by knowledgeable individuals. When properly created and validated, assessment tests should treat all applicants in the same, nonsubjective manner and should not discriminate on the basis of race, color, sex, national origin, religion, disability, or age.[3] The danger of prescreening personality testing arises when they are used for the sole purpose of weeding out candidates. Legal issues may arise if tests are inappropriately administered to protected categories of individuals for which the test was not designed or validated. Unfortunately, most candidates will have little choice in the matter, and if asked to take a prescreening test, you should do so willingly.

Integrity tests are designed to investigate a candidate's truthfulness and trustworthiness. Test questions generally focus on a candidate's past behaviors related to ethics or on interests and preferences. The answers provided by the candidate are used to predict future behavior and determine whether the candidate may be prone to unscrupulous actions in the workplace. In general, you will be more successful if you approach ethics or values-based questions by answering conservatively. For example, the answer to a question like, "Is it all right to steal food even if you are starving?" is always "No." Likewise, if you're applying for a position that involves any degree of customer service, and you answer "yes" to "I often lose my patience with others," you will probably not get the position. While all of us may lose our patience once in a while, under extreme circumstances, the key word here is *often*. In this situation you really can't blame an employer for not wanting to hire someone who has an issue with patience or temper—no one wants an employee who's going to go "postal" on their customers or staff.

WHAT TO BRING TO THE INTERVIEW

1. *Several copies of your resume*: just in case.
2. *Copies of college transcripts*: again, just in case.
3. *References*: a list of three to five references listing the name, title, name of employer, and your relationship to you. If you worked in a university setting and received cards or letters of appreciation from student clients or previous committee or service activities, make copies and bring them along to the interview. Remember to black out the client's last name for confidentiality purposes.
4. *Samples*: Bring examples of any special documents, projects, or presentations such as marketing proposals, professional publications, lesson plans, web page designs, computer programs, technical drawings, and research papers.
5. *Paper or digital portfolio*: Majors in art, communication, graphic design, architecture, education, engineering, computer science/IT, marketing, and sales should bring a portfolio (or refer the interviewer to a digital portfolio) that contains representative samples of their creativity, artistic range, lesson plans, research projects, computer programs, designs, and past projects.
6. *Evaluations*: Bring copies of evaluations you received of your work performance as an intern, researcher, clinician, student nurse, or student teacher.
7. *A tablet of paper*: Bring a notebook, legal tablet, or something to take notes on during the interview. You can also use it to jot down questions that you want to ask during the interview.

WHAT TO WEAR

Lack of appropriate attire immediately sends a negative signal to the interviewer. The impression you want to send is that you are a competent professional. Even if you have no formal work experience in your field, you can show them through your dress and mannerisms that you know how to fit in to the company's corporate culture.

The old rule of thumb is to dress up one level from what is typically worn on the job. Business and engineering majors should always dress a little more formally. This would entail a suit and tie for men, and a business suit (pants or skirt) for women. Men, if you're not sure what color suit/tie to wear, stick with a tailored white shirt and dark pants. A clean white shirt always has a crisp, clean look, and it'll go a long way.

Women can wear a skirt above the knee but not so short that you're tempted to tug and pull at it whenever you sit down. Limit the number of accessories you wear (no dangling earrings, bright green nail polish, heavy perfume)—you don't want your accessories to be a distraction.

Men and women may carry a briefcase, portfolio, or notepad but *not* a backpack (remember, you're not a student anymore).

In general it is always better to dress on the conservative side. If in doubt about what to wear, look in the mirror and ask yourself if your grandmother would approve of your choice of clothing and accessories. The exception to this rule is when you are applying for a position in a creative industry. When interviewing for positions in industries in which you would be expected to be up on the latest fashion trends or in industries where you are expected to demonstrate creativity, such as fashion design/merchandising, art, graphic design, or computer animation, it is permissible to show a little more of your personality through color or accessories.

Business Casual Attire Guidelines

- Err on the side of conservative.
- Present a tailored look.
- Wear a jacket, or at least bring one along with you.
- Do not wear tight, baggy, or sexually suggestive clothing.
- Tops should cover the abdomen.
- Tennis shoes and flip flops are not business casual.

Sometimes students will be told in advance to dress casually because they will be participating in activities with others. In that situation, you should dress comfortably, but not be dressed so casually that you look sloppy or careless.

BODY LANGUAGE

When it comes to acing your interview, it's important that your verbal and nonverbal communication are in perfect harmony. You don't want your body language to negate your words. Being cognizant of what your body language is communicating to others will only help your career success.

Employers want to hire people who are socially aware and confident. When you're in a job interview, you want all the attention focused on what you're saying. Refrain from toe tapping, bouncing your foot, nail biting, and anything else that could distract the other person.[4]

Salary.com has some excellent tips for using proper body language:

- *Make eye contact.* "We cannot underestimate the importance of eye contact. First of all, it's an unspoken way to establish a rapport and credibility. Second, it lets the other person know you're engaged and interested in what he or she is saying."[5] Look your interviewer in the eye. Fixing your eyes on the floor, on the wall, or on fixtures or furniture suggests boredom and lack of interest.

- *Sit straight in your chair.* Sit up straight in your chair with your feet planted firmly on the ground. Leaning back in your chair shows that you are too relaxed, don't take the job seriously, and are not an aggressive worker. Slouching in your chair says you are unprepared for either the interview or the job, and neither bodes well for you. Instead, lean slightly forward toward the interviewer, which conveys engagement and interest.

- *Keep your feet still.* It's best to keep your legs and feet uncrossed and still. Point your feet in the direction of your interviewer so he or she knows you are fully invested in the conversation.

- *Avoid nervous habits.* Everyone is nervous at the interview but you don't want to have your nervousness detract from your presentation. Find a comfortable position in your chair and try to avoid twitching or moving around excessively, nail biting, playing with your hair or jewelry, or excessive coughing or throat clearing. It's normal to feel a little nervous during an interview, but you have to do your utmost not to give it away.

- *Do not cross your arms.* Avoid sitting with your arms crossed tightly across your body because that conveys a lack of openness or anxiety. If you don't know what to do with your arms, try clasping your hands in your lap or lay them on your notebook.

- *Avoid excessive gestures.* Learn how to use minimal hand gestures for emphasis by practicing answers to potential questions in the mirror.

WHAT TO EXPECT IN AN INTERVIEW

In general, the interview can be divided into three parts[6]:

Part 1: The introduction. The first five minutes of the interview will involve casual conversation about the weather, the traffic, and/or any major sporting events that occurred over the weekend. These first five minutes are crucial. The way you look, present yourself and interact with the interviewer will establish his or her first impression of you.

Part 2: Establishing qualifications. Often the interviewer will begin by briefly describing the position before launching into a series of questions. Some people view this part of the interview as the interrogation section, but it doesn't need to be. Interviews should be a two-way conversation about your qualifications and the job in question. Allow the interviewer to lead the conversation, but don't be afraid to ask questions during the interview. Employers expect you to ask intelligent, thoughtful questions. Answer the questions by pulling examples from your resume, portfolio, or past experiences; comment favorably on your education, your past employers, and your plans for the future. Finally, come prepared with several good questions to ask the interviewer. Sitting there quietly shows that you are not invested in getting the position. Interviews for sales positions expect that you will try to "close the deal." Ask enough questions to gather the type of information you need to determine if this is a position you want to accept.

Part 3: Wrap-up. As the interview draws to a close, you will be asked if you have any other questions, or you may be told what the next step in the interviewing process is. For example, depending on your major, you may go on a tour of the facility, meet other staff members, participate in a "working interview," or simply shake hands and depart. If you are not sure what will happen next, then *ask.* Do not talk about money or benefits. Let the employer mention salary first. Broaching the subject first implies that you are more interested in money and perks than doing a good job.

In summary, most interviews will be conducted by one to three people, usually the HR person, your potential boss, and other people in the department where the position is housed. Interviews can last from 30 minutes to two hours, depending on the number of participants and the type of position. Don't be surprised if you are asked to come back for a second or third round of interviews. If you are unsure of what the interviewing format will be, ask the person who schedules your interview (preferably an HR person) if they can tell you about the participants, the format, and the length of the interview, so you can prepare and be at your best.

NINE

Interview Like a Pro

You never get a second chance to make a *first* impression.

—Anonymous

DURING THE INTERVIEW

To be successful in the interview you need to be able to talk about what you know, what you did, and what you can do for the employer in the future. Don't approach the interview by asking the employer to "give you a chance" or that "you just need a job" because there are just too many other well-qualified candidates to choose from in this job market.

Liz Ryan, an expert on the new-millennium workplace and a former Fortune 500 HR executive, offered this advice in a *Bloomberg Businessweek* article about interviewing: "Look at what you bring from the standpoint of what the employer needs. 'I need the job' is not compelling. 'Here's why you might need someone like me' is."[1]

When making your case to the employer or hiring manager, as when writing a research paper or giving a persuasive speech, you need to back your statements up with facts. Being able to *show* someone what you did is always more compelling than just *telling* them what you did. In the interview, your visual aids are your portfolio, and your "proof" is examples from your experiences at school or work. Whether you draw examples from class projects that you've completed or on-the-job/clinical experiences, use ones that demonstrate how you are a good fit for the position. If the interviewer is looking for teamwork skills, be sure to bring up a specific example of a senior-level project that you worked on with several classmates. You can demonstrate leadership using an example of running a club meeting or being the lead researcher in a chemistry project. Be concise in your answers and back them up with details, or tell a "story" that illustrates your point. Stories are easier to remember because they are more interesting and compelling.

Saying "Because I would be an asset to your company" in response to the often asked closing interview question "Why should I hire you?" is basically saying nothing if you don't have any evidence to back up your claim. A better response is, "Because I have the ability to explain complex algebraic principles to high school students in a way that they can understand."

If you think you're rambling in the interview, you probably are. When you catch yourself going on and on in response to a question, or running out of things to say (always a clue), quickly wrap it up by summarizing the "short" answer to the interviewer's question.

If you have a bad interview, get stuck on a question, or become confused, take a deep breath and think about what you want to say. Avoid the temptation to rush. What seems like an eternity to you is really only a split second to others. Regain your composure and ask for clarification if needed. Then answer the question as best you can and focus on the next question. After the interview, step back and learn what you can from the experience.

TYPES OF QUESTIONS OFTEN ASKED DURING THE INTERVIEW

A common ice-breaking question in the interview is, "Tell us something about yourself that is not on your resume." This line of questioning tends to throw many new graduates out of synch, so be prepared. Other prospective questions that you may be asked are: "What do you see as your greatest strength and your greatest liability?" "If I called your present supervisor about you, what would I be told?" "What have been your most significant achievement and your greatest regret?" My own personal favorite question is, "If you could become any animal you wanted to be, which animal would you be?" (Yes, I was actually asked this during an interview.)

Be prepared for interviewers to pose a series of predetermined questions designed to discover if you have the skills and necessary characteristics to succeed in the position. This line of questioning is based upon the old behavioral dictum, "The best predictor of future performance is past performance." In this type of interview, you may be asked to describe in detail a prior job or position, including responsibilities, accomplishments and failures, most and least enjoyable aspects of the job, and reason for leaving.

Behavioral-based interview questions examine past behavior as an indicator of future performance. Typically, the interviewer asks situational questions such as, "Tell me about a difficult situation you faced and how you resolved it," or, "Give me an example of how you would handle an irate customer," or, "Suppose you saw a client exhibiting these symptoms, what would you treat first?" or, "Could you tell us about a project you worked on in which the results did not turn out too well?" More elaborate behavioral-based questions ask the interviewee to solve a problem (typically seen in engineering or other technical fields). Some of the problems are virtually unanswerable such as, "How many balloons do you think could fill this room right now?" The questions are less about the actual situation and more about your approach to problem solving and the way that you handle stress. As you formulate your answer, break it down by explaining first the situation, then your approach and thought process when handling it, then the plan you implemented, and finally, how it was resolved.

At the conclusion of every interview an employer basically wants to know three things: (1) *can* you do the job, (2) *will* you do the job, and (3) are you going to *get along* with the rest of the staff. Your job is to make sure you have satisfactorily answered all of those "unasked" questions during your interview.

ILLEGAL INTERVIEW QUESTIONS

There are many good reference materials that deal with this subject in depth, so the topic won't be belabored here. In general, employers cannot discriminate against an applicant based on age, marital status/family status, religion, ethnic origin, disability, height, weight, arrest record, or military record. While an employer cannot ask you when you were born or how old you are, they can ask if you are over the age of 18. Likewise they can't ask you how much you weigh but they can ask if you can lift 50 pounds or more for a distance of 100 yards if that is a part of your job duties. An employer can ask if you were convicted of a felony or a particular crime, if you're authorized to work in the United States, and if you can perform the duties of your job with or without reasonable accommodations.[2]

Keeping these in mind, you probably will not want to voluntarily disclose personal information in the interview (like the fact that you were just married [woman] and plan to start a family soon). If you are asked an illegal question in the interview, it's your personal decision whether or not you want to answer the question, but I would advise you to redirect the question back by saying something like, "I am old enough (or young enough) to handle the responsibilities of the job," "I am able to do all of the requirements of this position," or "I am looking for a career and plan to give 110 percent to the job," and invite the interviewer to ask his or her next question. However, after the interview I would wonder whether the person who asked you the illegal question(s) is simply being ignorant, or is a reflection of the type of culture that exists at that company. Then decide if you *really* want to work in that type of environment.

HANDLING THE WEAKNESS QUESTION

The key in handing the "weakness" question is to spin your weakness into a strength. For example, if you find that you get frustrated with people who don't work as quickly or as thoroughly as you, what you are really demonstrating that you have high standards or are very efficient.

Although your interviewer wants to see that you are self-aware and are working to improve yourself, don't say something that would damage your candidacy, such as describing yourself as "perfectionist," "lazy," or a "procrastinator." I once interviewed someone who described her management style as "authoritarian." Needless to say, this was not the trait we were looking for and she did not get the job.

The one thing you don't want to say is that you have no weaknesses. Everyone has something they can improve on, especially new graduates. I often advise new graduates (if they can't think of anything else to say) to use their "lack of experience." But then back up that statement with something to the effect of "I know the fundamentals, but I just feel I need more exposure to . . . " or "But I'm sure that with some practice I will become proficient."

Being able to demonstrate how you've improved on a weakness, such as feeling anxious about public speaking, shows strength and maturity. You could say that taking Speech Com 101, where you were forced to make a speech each week, helped you hone your communication skills and become more comfortable speaking in front of people. Acknowledging how you've learned from the past shows that you are constantly looking to improve your performance.

Sometimes an interviewer will ask you about a technique or process with which you have no experience. In this case it usually doesn't pay to lie or try to bluff your way through the question. Be honest and say, "No, I don't have any experience with XYZ, but I am willing to learn." Or, "That program seems like it's very similar to AutoCAD, which I do know, so I feel confident that I'll be able to quickly pick it up." If you claim to be something you're not, chances are you'll be found out sooner or later and find yourself looking at job boards again.

QUESTIONS YOU SHOULD ASK

An interview is not an interrogation—it's a conversation, so come ready to ask some questions of your own. If not already discussed, you will want to know about the duties and responsibilities of the position. You may also want to know the management philosophy or supervisory style of the person you'll be working for. The answer to this question will give you an idea of what the interviewer will be like to work with, or work for, and what degree of autonomy exists, if any. A good follow-up to this question is to inquire about the staff turnover rate. Learning about staff turnover rates may give you some clues as to how well the management philosophy and supervision style has worked at that particular agency/institution.

Another area worth exploring is if the position has a probationary period, and if so, the length of that probation. Your follow-up question in this area should involve discovering what role the supervisor takes to help you get through the probationary period. Probationary periods can range anywhere from six months to three years.

You can also gain useful information about the company without directly asking. Look around you and notice your surroundings. While you're waiting for your appointment in the reception area, you can gage the "busyness" of the office by noting the volume of customers coming through the doors, the number of staff on duty, and the pace that people seem to operate at while performing their jobs. Are people friendly, relaxed, and enjoying their jobs, or are they uptight, overwhelmed, rude, or curt?

Consider asking some of these questions during an interview:

1. Who will I be reporting to? (A lead-in to who your boss is and where you fit in the organizational structure of the company)

2. How long has this position been open? (Not "Why is this position open?" which may put the interviewer on the defensive. This question can be followed up by, "Is the position open because you're replacing someone or is it a new position?")

3. How does the company balance work and personal-life issues? (A better way of asking than directly inquiring how the company treats its employees)

4. How would you describe the philosophy of the company or organization?

5. Can you tell me more about my responsibilities?

6. Describe a typical workday for me. (Provides insight into what your job is *really* going to be like)

7. What challenges might I encounter if I take this position? (Provides good insight into difficulties you may run into on the job, potential conflicts with staff, expectations of other departments, etc.)

8. What are the top three things that need to be immediately addressed in this job? (Provides clues to what will be expected of you when you walk in the door on your first day of the job)

9. What budget does this department operate with? (Provides clues to the fiscal soundness of the company. Will you have enough money to operate effectively in this job?)

10. How will my leadership responsibilities and performance be measured? By whom?

11. What are the department's goals, and how do they align with the company's mission?

12. Does this job usually lead to other positions in the company? (A softer way to ask about promotion potential)

13. Can you please tell me a little bit about the people I'll be working with? (Provides clues to who you'll be working with)

14. How would you describe the corporate culture here? (Listen closely to the way the interviewer answers this question for clues to the way the company runs its business and how it treats its employees.)

15. In your opinion, what is the most important contribution that this company expects from its employees? (Provides clues to what will be expected of you)

16. How does the company support and promote personal and professional growth? (This is the softer alternative to the "Do you offer tuition reimbursement?" or "Will I get a promotion?")

17. I'm glad to hear that I will be part of a team. How does the team generally operate? (Insight into the structure of the team and the dynamics of the people on the team)

If you really want to shine, ask to have a tour of the facility and/or meet the other members of the team/department that you'll be working with. Do not ask questions that may be perceived as negative or that will put the hiring manager on the defensive, such as, "Why did the company lay off three people last month?" or, "Why don't you have a tuition reimbursement policy?" Defensive questions will only throw up a red flag to a hiring manager who may peg you as a potential troublemaker.

Some experts recommend obtaining feedback during the interview by asking questions such as, "How am I doing go so far?" or "Are there any areas in which you feel I fall short of your requirements?" This is a tricky area, in my opinion. Just like asking an employer why you weren't hired for the position can place the interviewer in an uncomfortable position and end up backfiring on you, so can this type of question if not phrased correctly. When I was the chair of a search committee for a director of a grant program housed in my office, I was once asked by an interviewee, "What are the qualities are you looking for in a person in this position?" I found the question to be a bit bold and immediately felt uncomfortable, primarily because there *were* several key factors that I was looking for in a candidate (but I didn't want to tell her that). At the end of the interview, depending on how things went, it *might* be permissible to ask, "Are there any areas where I do not meet the qualifications of someone you're looking for in the position?" Still, I think a better way to obtain the information that you're looking for is by asking, "What skills/personality traits, etc., are you specifically looking for in this position?"

At the end of the interview smile, shake everyone's hand, and ask for their business cards so you can write a thank-you note later. If you are interested in the position, close by expressing your interest. Don't assume that the employer will know how much you want the job. Say something like, "I've really enjoyed meeting with you and your team, and I am very interested in this position," or "This sounds like a fabulous company to work for" or "I feel my skills and experience would be a good match for this position and I would really like the opportunity to show you what I can do." (Your comments will depend on the type of position you applied for.) If you're applying for a sales or marketing position, you will be expected to demonstrate that you can "close the deal." So, go ahead and close the interview by saying, "I think we have a great fit here. What do you think?" or "I know I can meet the demands of the position and would make an outstanding contribution to your team. What will it take to offer me the position?"

If the interviewer has not already told you, ask what the next steps in the interview process will be and how soon they anticipate finishing the search and making an offer.

Use the following checklists to help you prepare for any upcoming interviews.

Preinterview Checklist

1. I have the name, address, and telephone number of company.
2. I have the name of the person I will interview with.
3. I know how to get to the company.
4. I know what the company does.
5. I have my resume, references, and portfolio.
6. I have my list of questions.
7. I am dressed professionally.

Interview Checklist

1. I arrived for the interview at least 10 minutes early.
2. I greeted the receptionist in a friendly manner.
3. I stood and shook hands with a *firm* handshake.
4. I was appropriately and professionally dressed.
5. I did not slouch or fidget in my chair.
6. I did not smoke or chew gum.
7. I remembered to turn off my cell phone or left it in the car.
8. I gave the interviewer a copy of my resume and references.
9. I maintained good eye contact and attentive body language.
10. I was well prepared.
11. I showed an interest in the company and in the job.
12. I let the interviewer take the lead.
13. I gave clear and concise answers to questions.
14. I avoided slang expressions or using poor grammar.
15. I answered questions confidently.
16. I highlighted my strong points and gave examples.
17. I avoided criticizing former bosses or professors.
18. I was a good listener.
19. I maintained good eye contact.
20. I asked pertinent, intelligent questions concerning the job.
21. I asked when and how to follow up after the interview.
22. I thanked the interviewer for his or her time and consideration.
23. I let the interviewer know I was interested in the job.

AFTER THE INTERVIEW

Most hiring managers will tell you that only a small number of interviewees follow up with a thank-you letter. This is a technique that is rarely used, but it is quite effective and always appreciated. If you are really interested in the position, send a brief, handwritten thank-you note to the interviewer within 24–48 hours of your interview. Thank the interviewer for the opportunity to speak with him or her and reiterate your interest in the position. This is also your last opportunity to (briefly) include any relevant information that you forgot to mention in the interview.

I think waiting for a response about a job, once you have been interviewed, is the toughest part of the job search. Remember that an employer's time is not your time. They are not nervously waiting by the phone for a job offer—they have meetings, deadlines, and a host of other issues that may take precedence over filling a position. There are many things that can end up delaying the search—all of which are unbeknownst to the job seeker. If you were told that the process will be completed in two weeks, and three weeks have gone by without a response, then contact the employer and inquire about the status. It could be that something came up and they haven't had time to complete the search. Normally, I advise students to follow up every two to three weeks and continue to do so until the position is no longer open.

Private companies and institutions will usually respond quicker than public or state agencies. The search process at my college can take as long as six months by the time a search committee is formed, the required three levels of interviewing are conducted, the references are checked, and the board of trustees gives their approval. Many state agencies are unable to advertise an opening until the incumbent leaves the position, and many allow four to six weeks for applicants to submit their materials.

SALARY NEGOTIATION

The fact that you're a new graduate with limited work experience doesn't mean you do not have the right to be paid what you're worth. Generally speaking, salary should not be discussed until *after* you have been offered a job. If the employer brings up the subject during the initial interview, that's fine, but you should not be the first to bring it up.

When asked about salary, it is always best to state a range. This means you will need to know the current salary range in your profession for your level and in your hometown (or the city or town you plan in which you plan to work). Then you can respond, "I understand that an entry-level salary for this position is between A and B and I would expect to come in within that average."

To be able to intelligently provide a salary range or to begin any negotiating, you will need to know what the going salary rate is for your field and geographic location. Sites like Salary.com or JobStar.org can help you gather this information.

Researching the company, and knowing the high, low, and average salary for your job will put you in a better bargaining position. It also helps to know what you want in a job before you begin negotiating and determine the lowest salary that you are willing to accept.

Although most college graduates will not have the work experience or the technical expertise to warrant a higher salary, there are some exceptions:

- You have relevant work experience (such as an internship, summer job).
- You have a technical expertise that is highly in demand.
- You are an adult student and have previous work experience, such as management experience from a former career.
- You have a written job offer from another employer that offers a higher salary.

One of our computer aided drafting and design technology students, Jim, applied for a position with a midsize lumber company. Jim was an adult student who decided to make a career change later in life. Because he had some previous retail management experience, he was able to sell his value to the employer as a person who could quickly step into a management role in the company. As a result, he was able to start at a higher salary level than the entry-level salary that he was originally offered.

Conduct your negotiations respectfully, but don't push the issue if there's no room to budge. In a tight economy, sometimes a job is better than no job. If you're considering a position in another state, remember that the cost of living varies considerably in different parts of the country so make sure you factor in those costs.

Your salary is not always the only item that's negotiable. Other negotiable items include the starting date, signing bonus, moving expenses, paid association memberships, dates of performance reviews, performance bonus, retirement plan, medical insurance, profit sharing, and tuition reimbursement. Evaluate each item on the table and decide where you're willing to compromise before starting negotiations.

TEN

Choosing the Right Job Offer

Nothing is really work unless you would rather be doing something else.

—James Barrie

As I mentioned in an earlier chapter, my first summer job was at a pick-your-own strawberry farm. Most of us were high school kids who were hired for the strawberry season which roughly ran from June through July. We started at 7:00 (in the morning), worked seven days a week, and we loved it! Looking back on that experience now, I think what we enjoyed most was the camaraderie (and being outside in the summer sunshine, working on our tans).

One day a group of us were driven out to a field and asked to snip the blossoms off of the new strawberry plants. That was hard work and only served to reinforce our desire to go to college. We saw firsthand how hard the owners worked, and later asked ourselves how they could make enough money during the two short months of the strawberry season to sustain them throughout the year (I still wonder about that to this day). On the last day of the season, the owners threw a large picnic and let us swim in a rock quarry that was used for irrigation.

Even though I remember all of the fun I had at that job, I wouldn't want to do that job today. My point is that I enjoyed it back then because it appealed to me at the time. Everyone has their own definition of what makes a job satisfying or "fun." These individual differences and preferences are what make one job exciting to one, and boring beyond belief to another. In an ideal world, we would have a job that paid enough to meet our financial obligations and live whatever type of lifestyle we chose *and* that we truly enjoyed.

THE MEANING OF WORK

Work is the primary activity in most people's lives. Most of us spend more time at work than any other activity in life, except perhaps sleeping. Work is a place to use our talents, pursue interests, and develop our identity—all of which help us pursue our universal search for meaning. Beyond a means for acquiring food, shelter, and paying the bills, the ability to direct your own work, learn new things, collaborate with people who share your values and passions, and demonstrably contribute to an organization's goals have made work feel less like work. The context of work often changes as a person ages and moves through different stages of life. Marriage, children, job loss, aging parents, and illness are all factors that impact and may change the role of work in our lives.

Voices.com has a wonderful definition of work:

Work is meaningful, work is essential, and through our work we use our talents, gifts and strengths to the best of our abilities to serve other people, and through that service, we see a return that sustains us. (Stephanie Ciccarelli, cofounder of Voices.com)

For some people, work is not nearly as important as their home life (their children and family relationships), or their hobbies or other part-time pursuits. While their job may be enjoyable, it is not the center of their life but simply a way to pay the bills and allow them to pursue more important matters that exist outside of work. To others, work *is* their hobby or their passion and occupies a central role in their life.

Yale researcher Amy Wrzesniewski describes three distinct orientations people have toward work:[1]

- *Work as a job*: Seeing work as a source of income, satisfaction comes from hobbies and relationships outside work.
- *Work as a career*: Seeing work as a source of advancement, prestige, and status, job satisfaction comes primarily from continuing advancement. A person seeing work as a career will often dedicate extraordinary amounts of time and energy to their work.
- *Work as a calling*: Seeing work as a calling, a person derives satisfaction from the work itself because they believe it contributes to the

greater good. People with this orientation tend to experience more meaning from working.

Wrzesniewski also found that people who consider their jobs "callings" experience greater life satisfaction.

Existentialists suggest that meaning is connected to purpose in life and derived from one's answer to the question, "What is a good life?" Yalom maintains that the human being needs meaning to understand and interpret his or her experiences in the world and to define the values on which he can base his actions.[2]

In the 1950s and '60s the psychologist Frank Herzberg started looking at the issue of what people wanted from their jobs. He found that the factors that people attributed to satisfaction (achievement, recognition, the work itself, responsibility, advancement, growth) were different from what they attributed to dissatisfaction (company policies, supervision, relationship with supervisor and peers, work conditions, salary, status, security).[3] In other words, our reasons for *liking* our jobs have more to do with factors intrinsic to the work itself, and our reasons for *not liking* our jobs are usually related to the work environment.

Estelle M. Morin, Canadian psychologist, identified six characteristics that make work meaningful[4]:

- Social purpose: doing something that produces something meaningful to others
- Moral correctness: doing a job that is morally justifiable in terms of its processes and its results
- Achievement-related pleasure: doing a job that stimulates the development of one's potential and that enables achieving one's goals
- Autonomy: being able to use one's skills and judgment to solve problems and make decisions regarding one's job
- Recognition: doing a job that corresponds to one's skills, whose results are recognized and whose compensation is adequate
- Positive relationships: doing a job that enables making interesting contacts and good relationships with others

Pratt and Ashforth hypothesized that identity is also influenced by the meaning the individual finds in his or her work and work environment.[5] Thus work and the work environment are meaningful for an individual when he or she perceives a fit, a match, or alignment between his or her identity, work, and work environment.

In Daniel Pink's book *Drive*, he writes about the huge mismatch between what science knows and what business does. Businesses tend operate on the old operant conditioning model that the way to improve performance, increase productivity, and encourage excellence is to reward the good behavior and punish bad behavior.[6] He calls these motivational techniques "sticks and carrots." In other words, management will give their employees a big bonus if they make a profit or reach their production goals. Research has shown that the typical twentieth-century carrot-and-stick motivational techniques can actually decrease performance, crush creativity, crowd out good behavior, encourage cheating, shortcuts, and unethical behavior, become addictive, and foster short-term thinking. Science, on the other hand, has demonstrated that humans are actually motivated by the need for autonomy (intrinsic self-direction), mastery of a subject (the desire to get better and better), and having a purpose.

Daniel Pink also talks a lot about the concept of "flow," introduced by Mihaly Csikszentmihalyi, a Hungarian psychologist at the University of Chicago, in the 1970s. Flow is the mental state of operation in which a person in an activity is fully immersed in a feeling of energized focus, full involvement, and success in the process of the activity.[7] Surprisingly, Csikszentmihalyi found that people are much are more likely to reach a flow state at work than in leisure.

Harvard's Theresa Amabile has researched motivation levels of people on the job. She has found that the single greatest motivator is "making progress in one's work."[8]

Having a sense of autonomy has a powerful effect on individual performance and attitude. I know that when I became responsible for my own department my attitude shifted. I remember, in previous positions, hating having to work nights or weekends or traveling to some remote off-site location to register students. Mostly I hated being "told" that I had to do it. But when I became director I began looking at things a bit differently. I guess a sense of responsibility will do that. And as a result I found myself choosing to willingly coming in on a Saturday to work at an open house, or scheduling a late appointment to accommodate a working adult who wanted to make a career change. Paradoxically, because I had the freedom of choice (control over my department's activities and ultimately over my schedule), I *chose* to do those very events that I used to resent in earlier positions. Go figure.

As you work through your own personal definition of what work means, think about the larger picture. Assuming that you like your major, why did you choose the major? What do you hope to accomplish in your career? For many people, a job is a means to achieving other things such as: earning a lot of money, being able to afford a certain lifestyle, social status, power, influence. For others, it has a more internal or mission-based meaning: helping others, making a difference, pursing a cause. No single reason is better than another—it is purely individual.

People pursue college because they want more out of a job than just working from nine to five. Many of us have listened to our parents or grandparents talk about work as a duty or a way to support the family. They may not have liked what they did for a job but they did it anyway because it was a means to an end. Many of us went to college because we wanted to spend our lives doing something more than just working at a job. We want our work to have meaning, a sense of purpose, or a feeling of satisfaction at the end of the day. This is what most people envision as having a "career."

I think what Daniel Pink so eloquently describes in his book are the chief components of what we all envision that a "career" should be: being able to look forward to going to work, being totally engrossed in what you do so the hours fly by, being energized by your work, discovering new things, mastering a task, always moving forward, sculpting your craft, and building your reputation. When you have a job that you truly enjoy it won't seem like work and, as the saying goes, "the money will follow."

EMPLOYEE SATISFACTION

Research conducted by the Conference Board in 2010 indicated that less than half of American workers (45%) are satisfied with their jobs. In the Conference Board's first survey, conducted in 1987, 61 percent of workers said they were happy in their jobs.[9]

Employee satisfaction is a big deal to employers because the lack of it leads to lower levels of productivity, quality, and customer service, and to higher rates of absenteeism, tardiness, and employee theft. Recent research indicates that employees who find meaning in their work are more satisfied and more engaged, and in turn are more productive. Customers enjoy working with people who really enjoy their work and will return to that company to do business.

Job security appears to be an important factor in employee satisfaction. Given the recent state of the economy, more than half of U.S. workers feel their jobs are less secure now than they were a year ago. Approximately 70 percent of workers who feel their jobs are secure report happiness at work, but half of the workers who feel their jobs are in jeopardy are dissatisfied with their jobs. The takeaway from these statistics is that job security and employee satisfaction are connected, even though many workers are hanging onto their jobs only for a paycheck.[10]

Many employee satisfaction and retention surveys consider the following key aspects of employee satisfaction. Read through these and see if you agree:

- *Satisfaction with the work*: Regardless of salary and the people you work with, do you like the work that you do on a daily basis?
- *Level of empowerment/autonomy*: Employees are empowered to make decisions about and take responsibility for how they do their jobs. Employees may be given a company mission, vision, values, and goals for their department, but they have some control over how they perform their core functions and reach those goals.
- *Workplace culture*: Gallup research finds that engaged employees are likely to have a best friend at work. Overall, is the culture of the company is a good fit and do coworkers like and enjoy working with each other?
- *Pay and benefits satisfaction*: Are the pay and benefits acceptable to the employee? Does the company reward performance or find a way to tie in the interests of the employees with those of the employer?
- *Promotions/career advancement*: Employees feel as if they are encouraged to continue to develop their skills and careers. Employees are offered professional development opportunities and advancement potential.
- *Recognition*: Employers of choice provide regular feedback to employees about their performance, growth prospects, accomplishments, and areas needing improvement. One of the most powerful forms of feedback is employee recognition. At an employer of choice, recognition is regular, targeted to real successes, and used to reinforce positive, desired behavior.
- *Supervision/management*: Probably the greatest, single factor that can make or break a job is how well you get along with your boss. Do employees generally enjoy working for their boss?
- *Communication*: Information is shared with all employees at every level of the company. Employees feel that they know what's going on at their company.
- *Respect*: Employees feel that they are fundamentally respected by their bosses and coworkers. They have the opportunity to be heard and be involved in key areas of the company. Employees feel that their ideas and feelings are respected.
- *Work-life balance*: The company offers work-life balance initiatives such as flexible scheduling choices and maternity/family illness policies

that allow employees to work undistracted by the family/life events occurring outside of the workplace.

- *Fairness*: Perceptions of unfair treatment or a workplace that favors certain individuals over others for unknown, undefined reasons is an anathema to an employer of choice. Good employers fairly develop and apply policies, treat employees with the same regard and consideration, and make the workplace guidelines clear and enforceable across the board.

- *Understanding company mission and vision*: The company has a clear mission and vision. Employees understand, and generally are on board with that mission.

- *Job security*: Employees are reasonably certain that their employer is financially sound and are not concerned about losing their jobs.

- *Physical working conditions*: Are the working conditions safe, free from excess noise, dirt, or debris? Do employees have adequate facilities, equipment, and resources to do their job? Are working conditions in physical pleasant or ascetically pleasing surroundings?

WHEN WORK GOES BAD

I can talk quite knowledgeably about this topic—I've had a lot of jobs I didn't like. Most of them, as a matter of fact. I remember how trapped I felt in those jobs, sitting at my desk, watching the clock slow down and stretch unbearably between 4 and 5 o'clock. At that time I suffered from stress headaches and took a lot more time off work than I do now. Now I find that fatigue, illness, and even the occasional headache are much easier to tolerate in a job you enjoy than in one you don't.

Some people are bored to tears if their job is easy, monotonous, or boring. Others enjoy the predictable routine of that type of work. I found it numbing to work on an assembly line during summers when I was in college, doing the same task day after day. It all seemed so meaningless to me. Even though the people were nice, and I enjoyed the conversation flowing around me, it wasn't enough to make up for the monotony. I distinctly remember that they (management) wouldn't let us play the radio because they thought it would interfere with production. Actually, I think the opposite would have happened—we would have become energized if they had allowed us to listen to some upbeat music.

The downside to work is that it can cause stress, headaches, physical, and psychological ailments. According to statistics from the American Psychological Association, a startling two-thirds of Americans say that work is a main source of stress in their lives.[11] In fact, an American

Psychological Association survey found that 53 percent of workers reported fatigue due to work stress.

Stress isn't always bad. In small doses, it can help you perform under pressure and motivate you to do your best. But when you're constantly running in emergency mode, your mind and body pay the price. Seventy-hour workweeks have become the norm for many Americans. But this comes at a cost. Psychologist Connie Lillas uses a driving analogy to describe the three most common ways people respond when they're overwhelmed by stress[12]:

- *Foot on the gas*: an angry or agitated stress response. You're heated, keyed up, overly emotional, and unable to sit still.
- *Foot on the brake*: a withdrawn or depressed stress response. You shut down, space out, and show very little energy or emotion.
- *Foot on both*: a tense and frozen stress response. You "freeze" under pressure and can't do anything. You look paralyzed, but under the surface you're extremely agitated.

The effects of working are no longer just a male aliment. The incidence of alcoholism, heart attack, and lung cancer, illnesses previously seen only in men, is now on the rise in women. The negative effects of an emotionally charged or highly demanding career can also cause "burnout," which is characterized by emotional exhaustion, depersonalization, and decreased production. Burnout is seen more often in high-client-contact, emotionally draining careers such as special education, nursing, and social work.

FACTORS TO CONSIDER IN A JOB

An AfterCollege 2011 survey of college students, graduates, and alumni ranked the following factors when considering a job[13]:

1. *Work-life balance*: This class of graduates is leaning toward a less hectic style of working that leaves room for personal time.
2. *Salary*: A good paycheck is still very important to college students and recent graduates. (Benefits came in a close fourth.)
3. *Location*: Geography as an important consideration in the overall job package (ranked as the second least important factor).
4. *Reputation*: This plays a big part in the overall ranking of a company in the job search process. A poor public perception will most likely become a big deterrent for potential candidates.

In addition to the factors identified in the AfterCollege survey, here are some additional factors that you may find important in determining your best work environment:

- *Mission*: The mission of the organization may be important to you, the way it conducts business, the type of clientele, the products it produces, or the services it provides.
- *Motivation*: Think about what motivates you—is it achievement, competition, status, or money? Or perhaps it is seeing the results of a job well done, or the satisfaction of knowing that you helped someone out. Some people love detail work, or pride themselves on their ability to produce or design something. Other people are highly creative and thrive in an environment that lets them push the envelope of skills or design, while still others find security in the routine of daily tasks. Think about what elements would have to be present in a job to make you want to get up and go to work each morning.
- *Relationships*: For some people it is very important to enjoy the people that they work with. What type of relationship do you want to achieve with the people you work? Are you energized by a few intimate relationships, or do you need relationships with many people? There is some level of customer service in any position, whether customers, clients, or people in another department. Will your position involve front-line customer contact or media exposure? Or will you be interacting with only a few key members of a team or with people on an individual basis?
- *Physical office environment*: Do you function best in a noisy, busy environment with lots of interaction with people? Or in a quiet, comfortable space that allows you to think or work, uninterrupted, for long periods of time. Would you prefer working in an office, a cubicle, or an open environment? If you're not sure, think about what type of study environment that works best for you—that may provide clues to your preferred work environment.

Accepting a job offer is a personal decision and one that only you can make. You may want to use a simple pro-and-con list when determining whether or not to accept a position. Another commonly used exercise is to list all of the characteristics you want in a job in one column, then list all of the characteristics that the job offers in a second column and compare the two lists.

DECREASE THE RISK IN ACCEPTING A JOB

There is always some inherent risk involved when you take a new job because you never really know what the job is like until you get there. But that doesn't mean you can't do a little preliminary research to get all of the facts before making a decision.

Here are some ways to research your potential or future boss:

1. Read though company bios. Visit the company website and for an "About us" section.

2. Google the individual's name or name of company and see what information comes up. You may find their personal website, blog, social networking profiles, or news articles. You may even stumble across some company photos that will give you insights into the company's culture.

3. Read company reviews, industry profiles, and financial reviews.

4. Use social networking sites. Find your company or your boss on LinkedIn or follow them on Twitter. You can learn about the person's past job experience and recommendations to get a sense of his or her management style, etc.

Other factors to consider are the stability, profitability, or security of the company. For government or social services, and some educational positions, you may want to inquire about the funding source and how stable that funding is. Many university positions are funded by outside grants, internal grants, or fees generated by clients. Freelance positions generally pay a higher salary but may not include benefits. In addition, if taxes are not taken out of your earnings, it will be up to you to pay estimated quarterly state, federal, and Social Security "self-employment" taxes.

Some people are so worried about making the wrong choice that they make no choice at all. There is no crystal ball to predict how our lives will turn out; the only thing we can do is make the best decision we can with the information we have at the time. Even if you decide to take this job and it doesn't turn out the way you hoped, it will have given you experience and references, and allow you to move on to your next position. It's all part of the journey.

ELEVEN

What to Do When You Can't Find a Job

Fall seven times, stand up eight.

—Japanese proverb

Looking for work *is* your job right now: finding openings, following up on leads, going through interviews, and doing lots of waiting. Looking for a job, especially that first job, is never easy—and it's even harder when the job market seems to be working against you. To avoid job search burn-out, devote only a couple of hours a day to the process. If you are starting to feel discouraged or depressed, take a break and do something totally unrelated like taking a walk along the dike, shooting hoops at the gym, meeting friends for lunch, or riding your bike along a lakeshore path. When you come back you'll feel refreshed and ready to start again. Although it's easy to become discouraged and even feel a bit depressed after an unsuccessful day of job searching without some tangible results, don't give up—your persistence will pay off.

TROUBLESHOOTING YOUR JOB SEARCH

One mistake many young job seekers make is to think that if they apply for a job and get an interview, they're going to get the job. So they put their job search on hold while they're waiting for one job to play itself out before searching for the next opening. In a tight economy, it may take hundreds of applications, and many interviews, to get one job. A better approach is to keep your options open and continue to apply until you accept an offer. Then be professional and inform the other positions that you are no longer interested in their openings.

If you're being invited in for interviews, that's a good sign. But if you're not getting the job, then you may need to work on your interview skills:

- Focus on improving your interview skills by doing practice interviews. Ask your career services if they can offer suggestions or do a mock interview with you.
- Review your dress, appearance, and body posture with a friend or career services staff member. Then correct any speech pattern or body language issues.
- Practice formulating better responses to interview questions.
- During the interview listen carefully before speaking and answer questions succinctly.

If you are finding openings but not being invited in for interviews try these tactics:

- Give your resume a tune-up. Make an appointment with your former career services office (many offer services for alumni) or consult with a career coach. Review your interviewing presentation and job search strategy. If nothing else, the verification you receive that you have been doing everything right will help.
- Use a stronger summary statement; highlight results.
- Practice saying your introduction statement aloud. It should express what you want people to remember most about you. Aim to keep your introduction 15–30 seconds long.
- Network for recommendations.

If your job search is not producing results, then your technique may be the problem. Many students and alumni who have difficulty finding a job simply do not know where to look. (Review chapter 4, "Where to Look for Job Openings.") Here are some suggestions to improve your technique:

- Target your resume to each position. When asked what kind of job they're looking for, I hear many discouraged job seekers say, "I'll take *anything*—as long as it's a job." This is a common job search theme, and it probably has its roots in the notion that if you're flexible, more jobs will be available. But employers aren't looking for "anyone who can do anything." Job postings cite a specific job title and the skill sets the employer is hoping to find. Be specific and target your resume to each position

- Adjust the amount of time you are spending on any one search tactic. For example, you may be spending too much time focusing on job boards and not enough applying directly to company websites. It pays to use all available methods to find openings—general and niche job boards, company websites, newspaper ads, professional organizations, trade journals, career services postings, and social media.

- Network to gain information about unadvertised jobs.

- Consider that the job pool in your geographic area is too small or dried up. If that is the case, then you may need to look outside of your immediate geographic area and apply for positions you would otherwise consider "too far away." Consider alternate transportation methods or carpooling, to defray the cost of gas.

- Be proactive. Make it a point to talk to at least one unsolicited employer a day, whether that employer has an opening or not. If they're impressed, they may offer you a position. Even if they don't have a vacancy, they may know of other employers who do. It's all about getting out there, finding unknown opportunities, and taking advantage of them.

- Be flexible and strategic. If you are unable to find a full-time position, take a part-time, temporary, consultant, or per diem position. Then use that position to build your skills and experience while continuing to look for a better opportunity. Remember, in a tough economy having *a* job is better than having no job at all.

- Consider registering with a temporary help service agency such as Manpower, One Source, or Kelly Services (check your local yellow pages under Employment Services) or register with a permanent staffing agency. Choose a staffing agency that charges the employer, not you. Contact career-specific recruiters (many advertise on the Internet or announce positions on LinkedIn). Sometimes temporary assignments lead to permanent positions. In any event, temporary assignments will bring in some welcome cash in the meantime and you will gain more skills, experience, and references to put on your resume.

- If you suspect that lack of experience is the culprit and you didn't participate in an internship or some other work while you were attending college, seek out a consulting assignment, go to a temporary agency, or apply for an internship or externship after graduation to get some real-world experience.

There are jobs in every major—the trick is to know where to look for them. If there are no jobs in your major in your hometown, that doesn't mean there are no jobs *anywhere*. It just means you will have to expand your geographic area and look for openings in another city or in another state. When the economy is poor, you need to go where the jobs are. Taking a job in another part of the state or in another state altogether doesn't mean that you have to stay there forever. After a couple of years, when the economy improves you will have two or three years of experience under your belt and will be in a much better position to compete for positions than you are now.

PART-TIME, TEMPORARY, OR CONTRACT WORK

If you're not able to find a full-time job, consider taking a part-time, per diem, or temporary position in your major. One of the positive consequences of our recent recession is a surge in the number of opportunities for freelancers, contractors, sole proprietors, consultants, temps, and self-employed workers. Some of these part-time openings exist because companies had to lay off employees and didn't want to hire back full-time employees until the economy improved, so they may lead to full-time when the economy improves.

In a poor job market, some students find that the way to survive is by holding down one or two part-time jobs. Retail stores, hospitals, and delivery companies are a good source of part-time jobs, and many of them even offer benefits if you work over 20 hours per week. The benefit of part-time or temporary work is, in addition to earning a paycheck, you're gaining that valuable "work experience" that's so needed on your resume.

Some students hesitate to take a position that is not in their major because they're afraid it will reflect negatively on them when they interview for a position in their field. In a poor economy, any job is better than no job. Focus on skill development and remember that you can always use that job to showcase examples of customer service, sales or marketing, or even leadership skills. Taking any kind of job, while continuing to look for a job in your major, can also demonstrate to an employer your determination, work ethic, and initiative. It's all how you spin it!

ALTERNATIVE OPPORTUNITIES IN YOUR MAJOR

The laws of supply and demand govern most majors, and job availability is often cyclical. Years ago, nursing was not the highly sought after major it currently is. But even nursing positions became competitive as hospitals began cutting back and even laying off staff because of budget difficulties. Nursing graduates who wanted that coveted first-shift job in a hospital setting needed to look at other health care alternatives such as home health, private clinics, doctor offices, correctional institutions, and public schools.

Another example is education. Currently, the job outlook for public school teachers is pretty poor (except for math and science teachers). However, schools are still going to need teachers to teach our children, and education jobs will rebound again in a few years when state budgets become more stabilized and more baby boomer teachers retire. In the meantime, education majors may need to look at the private education sector (parochial schools, private residential schools, charter schools, cyber high schools), Teach for America, international teaching options, early childhood education centers, or state or federally funded grant programs that provide academic support services to at-risk or special populations of students, or migrate into tutoring or educational sales.

If you're not able to find a traditional position in your major, think outside the box and look for nontraditional employers or related opportunities to keep you employed in your major.

GO BACK TO SCHOOL

Another option is to go back to school to earn another certification or continue to graduate school to earn a master's degree. To continue with the education example, teachers, with a master's degree, could specialize in special education, reading, school psychology, or school counseling. In addition, they would be eligible for a number of positions at a college or university such as in the learning support center (tutoring center), student support services, or even positions in the admissions, student activities, academic advising, development, or alumni offices.

CONSIDER VOLUNTEERING

Even if you can't find work in your field, you need to keep building experience so consider volunteering. Most people hesitate to exercise this option because, well, it involves working without being paid. But think of it as an investment in a future job, or an opportunity to develop or enhance the skills that will make you more marketable. If you're looking to get into accounting, for example, contact certified public accountants in your area to see if they'd be willing to take you on as an unpaid intern to help around the office (especially around tax time). Volunteering can keep you connected with professionals in your field, which may lead to a potential career. You'll learn new skills and make new contacts that you can later use as references, and your resume will show employers that you're genuinely interested in the field.

A graduating CIS student told me that he was going to volunteer to create a website for a local nonprofit company if he wasn't able to find a job. He reasoned the experience not only would give him something productive to do but also would give him some valuable references and another real-world example for his portfolio. He got a job not long afterward.

WHEN YOUR SKILLS ARE PERCEIVED AS BEING STALE

This may be a problem for students who take too much time off after graduation, especially in technology or the health care field where changes occur daily and skills deteriorate without use. I recently worked with Julie, a nursing alumnus, who took care of ill family members for two years after graduation. When Julie came to see me, the situation had resolved itself, and she was ready to reenter the workforce. But when Julie began applying for jobs she got little or no response. Luckily for her, a nursing recruiter finally explained that because Julie had been out of the nursing field for two years, her skills were perceived as "dated." Although Julie felt her skills were as sharp as ever, she was perceived as being stale by others in the marketplace. Julie immediately enrolled in a couple of refresher courses at our community college. Although she wanted to work in a hospital setting, she took several part-time, temporary positions with a nursing staffing agency to regain the impression she was up-to-date and employable. Eventually, she landed a second-shift position at a local hospital.

If you think employers may perceive you as being out-of-date, you may want to do the following:

- Take a refresher course at your local college.
- Obtain an advanced certification to demonstrate your relevancy in the field.
- Volunteer or work part-time, or on a per diem or temporary basis to gain some current experience.
- Stay busy, and productive, while looking for work. Demonstrate continued growth, learning, and achievements to fill the gap on your resume.

IF ALL ELSE FAILS

If you have tried your very best to find a job and still can't get one, there are still a few options left if the bills are starting to pile up:

- Reduce your monthly bills by moving in with a friend or even moving back home with your parents. Remember, it's only temporary.

- Register at a temporary help company or a staffing agency. This is a great way to bring some cash into the house if even if the job is not in your field. Explain that although you would prefer a job in (whatever it is), you would be willing to take anything in the meantime. Some of these positions do lead to permanent positions, and some staffing companies even offer their employees benefits. The key is to be flexible.

- Go back to a previous employer and ask for a job. If the pizza place you worked at while in college liked you back then, you may have a real shot at getting some hours now.

- Call your student loan lender and ask for a payment deferment or loan consolidation.

- Many communities have a locally based, free credit counseling service that can help you manage your bills and give you advice on how to reduce spending. This is not to be confused with a consumer credit counseling services affiliated with a bank or credit card company.

CHECK YOUR ATTITUDE

Attitude is the one factor that, no matter what else is going on in your life, you do have control over. Even though you just lost your girl/boy-friend, misplaced your purse, or smashed up your brand-new car (which would be enough to make anyone depressed), how you choose to view that situation and how you choose to react to that situation is up to you.

Based on employer feedback, attitude is a major factor in hiring decisions. Employers seek candidates who are enthusiastic, confident, motivated, and approach new situations with a "can do" attitude. When all other factors are equal, attitude will win out. Put yourselves in the employer's shoes. If you were hiring someone to sell a product that you worked hard to produce, would you choose someone who appeared like they could care less about you or your company, or someone who showed a genuine interest in your company and its products, and was excited about the prospect of working for you? Employers are only human—having a genuine interest in them and their company not only appeals to their human nature, but they will extrapolate that eagerness into hard work, ambition, and enthusiasm for the job.

If you are having a difficult time finding a job, it is imperative that you appear outwardly positive in every interview even though you may feel frustrated or discouraged. Poor attitudes come through in telephone calls and in interviews. Smile into the telephone, or during the interview, and inject some enthusiasm into your words. If you appear disinterested or unmotivated in the interview, a situation where everyone is expected to be on his or her best behavior, then an employer is logically going to wonder if you're going to act that way on the job. In a weak job market, employers will quickly eliminate any job seekers who appear desperate or negative because there are so many other candidates to choose from. However, it usually doesn't pay to overact. Employers are not fools and most will be able to detect false enthusiasm. Be yourself, but be your most upbeat and interesting self.

THE CONCEPT OF MENTAL TOUGHNESS

I think job seekers need to have a degree of mental toughness to survive the job search process. What makes looking for a job so mentally and physically draining is that you go through a roller coaster of emotions, from being excited about a job prospect to crashing down in despair when you don't get the job. Then when the next interview rolls around, you have to mentally pull yourself "up" for the next interview. Successful job seekers need to remain positive and persevere. That's why the concept of mental toughness is so appropriate in the job search.

Think about the quarterback who fumbles the ball or throws an interception in a critical play of a down. The worst thing he can do is become flustered and throw another interception.[1] Good quarterbacks put the previous plays behind them and go out and focus on the task at hand (throwing another touchdown). Learning to forget about a bad play and move on to the next one is an attitude that helps football players win games and, I believe, will go a long way to helping job seekers progress from one job interview to the next with confidence and optimism. Try not to take job rejections personally. People do not get jobs for many reasons—most have nothing to do with them personally. There is only so much you can do to get another person to hire you for a job, so learn what you can from the experience, and continue on to the next job interview. Just like the football player who drops the ball but needs to go back out and successfully make the next play, a certain amount of mental toughness is needed when searching for a job. You must be able to shake off the disappointments and focus on to the next job interview.

To keep your attitude up during the frustration of the job search, find something to do for a couple of hours that will take your mind off of looking for a job. Go for a run, work out in the gym, swim, or smack some tennis balls around the court. Physical activity is a natural stress reliever. Others find relief in talking with friends, going out to lunch, reading, watching a movie, or hiking in the woods. Find whatever it is that calms and refreshes you and do it. If you find that you are feeling depressed and discouraged to the point where you can't think straight or can't motivate yourself to do anything but sit around or sleep, then it's time to seek the help of a psychologist or mental health professional.

Some people find that relaxation techniques or meditation help them through that long, anxious waiting period between applying for and getting a job. Program your mind for success by saying positive affirmations, and expect that you *will* be successful. Building mental job toughness is like building muscle—you have to work at it in order to make it stronger.

Instead of dwelling on *getting* the job, shift your perspective and put more emphasis on the *process* of finding the job. Look for small, measurable gains. Set several small goals a day, such as identifying a job opening, getting a job lead from a friend or networking contact, successfully following up on job leads, applying for a job, making a new network contact, and going on job interviews. Document your activity on a daily basis. This not only will keep you organized but will provide some tangible feedback that will help you see what you have accomplished.

JUST KEEP SWIMMING

Robert Shindell, president and "The Career Doctor" at ILostMyJob.com, wrote an inspirational article called "Job Hunting in an Economic Downturn," which was published on CareerCenterToolbox.com. In the article, he uses a wonderful metaphor from the movie *Finding Nemo* and applies it to the job search process.[2]

If you are familiar with the film, you'll recall that Marlin is on a quest for his son, Nemo, who was caught by fishermen and ended up in an aquarium. On his quest, Marlin meets up with Dory and the two embark on the search for Nemo.

Marlin is basically a defeatist. He always sees the bad in every situation. Dory, however, is just the opposite. She always sees the positive. In one scene, when Marlin has given up hope of ever finding his son, Dory starts singing a song that she made up: "Just keep swimming . . . Just keep swimming . . . Just keep swimming."

Marlin wants to give up. He cannot see that there could be a positive outcome to his situation. Dory, on the other hand, remains focused and is positive that if they just keep swimming they will reach their goal. And eventually they do.

The lesson of this story is that it's so easy to become "Marlin" when you're looking for a job, especially in this economy. But when you encounter negativity and rejection after rejection, you need to take Dory's advice and "just keep swimming."

REMAIN OPEN TO POSSIBILITIES

Keep your eyes open for possibilities. Being open to possibilities suggests that you adopt an active, searching mentality. Because we don't know what possibilities may be "out there," continue to network, seek out openings, and go on interviews. Sitting at home will not create possibilities.

Some new grads discard job opportunities solely based on the job description. This is a big mistake. If you have at least 75 percent of the qualifications listed, apply for the job. Even though the description may not seem like your "dream job," always go on the interview when invited. When my husband and I were looking for a house, I saw our current home listed in the newspaper but quickly dismissed it because it wasn't a particularly good picture and was taken in the middle of winter. My husband, on the other hand, took the time to read the description and called the realtor. When we looked at the house and property, we quickly realized it was everything we were looking for in a home. Had it been up to me and my quick dismissal of the listing in the paper, we would have never found the home that we enjoy to this day. The takeaway here is that job descriptions may or may not accurately reflect the quality of the actual job. So don't be so quick to disregard any openings before you get the facts.

Other students are so bombarded with negative news about the economy and the job market that they feel discouraged and stop trying because they feel job searching is futile. Today's job search is more about perseverance than anything else. It doesn't matter how many times to apply or interview for jobs—you need only *one* good job offer.

MAINTAIN PERSPECTIVE

Prepare yourself as best as you can before stepping into the interview. Understand that there are lots of people looking for jobs today. If you aren't selected, don't take it personally (you could have been up against someone with more experience or even the boss's nephew). Some experts recommend calling the hiring manager back and asking how you could have improved your interviewing performance. I'm not sure I agree with this strategy—asking someone why you weren't hired places that person in a very difficult position. Most interviewers either are restricted by company policy on what they can disclose or are afraid of possible legal ramifications. So I wouldn't do it. A better approach is to ask someone who can critique your answers and presentation style and provide you with constructive feedback and advice, such as a career services or HR professional.

Learn what you can from each interviewing experience, make changes where possible, and then move on. Practice is the key to successful interviewing. Each interview gives you more experience in handling difficult interview questions, which in turn will make you feel more confident about your abilities, which will enable you to perform better in the next interview. View each interviewing opportunity for what it is—a new opportunity to get a job!

Last but not least, do not give up. Although it may take longer than you expect, eventually the right position will come along.

TWELVE

Surviving Your First Year on the Job

Toto, I've a feeling we're not in Kansas anymore.

— Dorothy in the *Wizard of Oz*

Many of you are members of the Millennial generation—the 88 million people born between 1977 and 1997. Currently your generation comprises roughly 35 percent of the U.S. workforce but is projected to make up 47 percent of the workforce by 2014.[1] You have been described as enormously clever and resourceful, hardworking, and possessing the tools and gadgets to get things done.

In a ComeRecommended.com post, Elizabeth Short wrote, "As a member of Gen Y, I possess many of the same characteristics as other members: I am always attached to some sort of technology, my family comes first, and I work hard for everything."[2] However, she takes offense at the stereotype that Gen Yers have a "sense of entitlement" and writes, "Let me start off by saying a majority of Gen Y members do not feel a sense of *entitlement*! This bothers me when I read or hear people say that word, because we understand that things aren't going to be handed to us and we have to work hard if we want to succeed."

I tend to agree. In fact, I heard the same complaint some 25+ years ago when I was first starting out in my career. The "entitlement" complaint seems to surface with the introduction of each new generation into the workplace.

As the Millennial generation's presence begins to be felt in the workplace, there will undoubtedly be some generational "growing pains" from members of previous generations. More and more members of the baby boomer generation are delaying retirement because of economic necessity or the need to remain active and useful. As a result, we will continue to see an increase in the number of older workers in the workplace. Unique to today's workplace is the possibility of seeing workers from as many as four different generations at one company. Both younger and older workers alike will have to learn how to deal with and respect the intergenerational differences arising from each generation's respective ages, life experiences, work values, and familiarity with technology.

MOVING FROM COLLEGE TO CAREER

Your ability to collaborate with individuals from different cultures and backgrounds, to cooperate with diverse personalities, to be a team player, and to work on projects with strict deadlines will all be put to the test in your first job. Staying organized and managing your time will remain crucial. The good news is that your college experience has provided you with these types of skills. The trick is to transfer them to your new work environment.

College life gave you incredible flexibility when dealing with classes and time schedules. Unfortunately, the work world is not that tolerant or flexible. They will expect you to be at work at 8:00 A.M. (or earlier) and work straight through (with requisite lunch and breaks, of course) until it's time to go home. Your boss will not care that you are not a "morning person," and he or she will not be happy that you missed that 8:00 A.M. breakfast meeting because you overslept or your car didn't start. You can probably get away with one lapse, but frequent "excuses" will lead to disciplinary write-ups and, eventually, dismissal.

Adjusting to the work time clock is a rude awakening for some students. There will be no vacation breaks or summer vacation. You will have to accrue your vacation time like everyone else. Sometimes you'll be asked to come in early and work late or even work on weekends—it's all just part of the job.

The University of Tennessee at Knoxville Career Services offers some wonderful advice about bosses:

Your boss is not like your college professors and should not be viewed in a similar manner. The professor had all the answers, encouraged argument and debate, laid out guidelines to assignments (generally well ahead of a due date), and was expected to be fair and objective. Your boss, on the other hand, often will send you to get the answers, will discourage arguments, will be vague as to how to complete a task, and often will come up with last-minute assignments, unclear priorities, and vague directions. The sooner you can accept this change from professor to boss, the greater your chance at success.[3]

Many graduates breathe a sigh of relief knowing that there will be no more final exams. Although you won't be expected to take quizzes and tests on your job, you will continue to be evaluated throughout your professional career. Evaluation on the job comes in the form of annual or semiannual performance reviews. In addition, many positions, like my own, require annual goals and objectives and outcomes assessments. The consequence of a poor review may be termination or loss of a bonus, raise, or promotion. In some professions such as in accounting, finance, health care, engineering, or law, the cost of making errors on the job may lead to serious consequences, even the difference between life and death. There is a need for continued evaluation—if only to ensure professional competency. Self-appraisals and formal performance reviews, if done properly, can be mechanisms for professional and personal growth and improvement. In some industries such as higher education, formal evaluation happens less frequently as one reaches certain milestones in one's career. Hopefully, through the process of continuous improvement, you will be able to develop a solid work history of success on the job and a strong professional reputation.

College is a place that lends itself to pursuing one's individuality, and discovery of self. In the workplace, the atmosphere and setting is much more formal and there are specific rules regarding dress and behavior that you must quickly adapt to if you hope to survive your first job. These rules are particularly evident in corporate settings. Some companies expect that their employees will wear a button-down shirt and tie while others require a uniform. If you work in the IT industry for a company like Google, for example, your work setting may be more informal and flexible. In these environments, the corporate culture is to allow creativity and individual expression, and employees can come and go as they please and dress in comfortable clothes.

Work environments vary greatly according to industry, company culture, and the nature of the job itself. Pay attention to the corporate culture at your job. Learn how things work within your company. Are relationships formal or friendly? Does everyone arrive early and stay late? Are lunch hours short or nonexistent? What type of behavior and dress is expected of those in management or administration? I used to work at an institution where the administrative *look* was a blue suit and silver hair.

Depending on the company that you work for, how well you fit in to the corporate culture can make a difference in how successful you will be in that job.

If you're accustomed to texting and checking your Facebook account during class and you're about to enter the world of work, you should be aware of workplace policies regarding personal use of the Internet and electronic devices. Security of company information is often a huge concern to employers. Unauthorized access to classified programs, leaving a company computer unattended, sharing passwords, or downloading forbidden programs is a very big deal at some companies. Be aware that your online activity may be scrutinized by sophisticated software programs, and depending on your company's Internet policy, unacceptable behavior can result in termination. Save your personal e-mail and text messaging for off-work hours and understand your company's policy about using e-mail and the Internet for personal use during work hours.

One challenge that many new graduates have difficulty with when they begin their careers is starting at the bottom rung on an organization's administrative ladder. When you graduated from college you were at the top level—a senior, with all of the rank and privileges that came with seniority. In the work world you will have to start all over again, proving your worth and working your way up the administrative ladder. This is where attitude will propel you farther than anything else. You want to be the go-to person who has a positive attitude and is willing to do whatever it takes to get the job done. That includes rolling up your sleeves and pitching in to stuff envelopes so the bulk mailing for your upcoming publicity event gets out on time. According to Nancy Barry, author of *When Reality Hits: What Employers Want Recent College Graduates to Know*, if someone asks you to do something that causes you to think "You want me to do *what*?" smile and say, "I'll be more than happy to do that."[4]

NEW-JOB BLUES

Everyone who's ever started a new job goes through the "new-job blues" until they acclimate to their new job. You'll probably feel overwhelmed in the first few days or weeks of your job, because everything will be new to you. Just finding the copier and the cafeteria will seem like major accomplishments at first. Make notes or a cheat sheet about people, positions, and important procedures like filling out the travel reimbursement form. If you have a secretary, make that person your best friend. Secretaries know everything and everyone and can make your life so much easier (or more difficult) depending on how you treat him or her.

Again, most people feel overwhelmed during the first couple of days on a new job. You may even have some doubts creep in about whether or not you should have taken this job or if you can cut it at all. Give yourself a chance to get adjusted and realize that you are going through a steep learning curve—from a college classroom to learning your colleagues' names to company policies and navigating the corporate culture. Remember what it felt like when you first went to college? Things got better then, and they will get better now. You will have to pay your dues in your first job too, so settle in and enjoy the ride.

You'll probably have a number of things to get done that have been handed to you by your supervisor, and possibly by several different people, depending on your situation. Learn to prioritize. If you're not sure what task or project should receive priority, ask your boss which is the most important task or which should be completed first. "Assuming" will generally get you into trouble, so if you aren't sure what to do—*ask*! And unless there's a specific deadline, no one is expecting you to get everything done in the first day or week.

As in the interview, people will be making impressions based on meeting you during the first few days. Be professional, be on time, and treat *everyone* with respect and friendliness. You haven't learned the office politics yet and don't want to make any mistakes. Eat lunch in the cafeteria so you can meet people. Lunch break is a social time, and building relationships at your office is very important. Not only will you be happier if you like the people you work with, but it's also important for your job security. Watch your use of personal e-mail and social media. Pull your own weight; offer to help others (they may be very willing to return the favor when you need it). Remember that the only way to build respect is to do a good job.

Time management is one skill that can transfer from college to your career—juggling multiple projects, knowing how to prioritize and balance short- and long-term projects, staying on top of a project until completion, and following up with clients in the same way you kept up with readings and assignments in class. Just as understanding how you learned best in school helped you succeed academically, so will understanding how you *work* best help you succeed on the job.

View your first year on a new job as a transition stage that lasts from the time you accept your job until the end of your first year. In this stage you're not a college student anymore, but you're not really a professional yet, either. However, it is this stage that can make or break the early part of your career. During this transition period try to find someone who has been around for a while, is respected by others, and is willing to answer questions and give you advice when needed, especially when it comes to the unwritten rules governing office behavior.

STRATEGIES FOR SUCCESS ON THE JOB

According to employers polled in an April 2005 survey by CareerBuilder.com, the top four mistakes new grads make in their first 90 days on the job are showing up late, being negative, spending too much office time on personal business, and not asking for help when they need it.[5]

Michigan State University offers some good strategies for success on the job.[6] Here are some of their suggestions plus a few of my own:

- Don't come in with a "know-it-all" attitude—that really turns people off.
- In the workplace, what you do affects others. If you get behind, it becomes a problem for your team, coworkers, boss, and anyone reporting to you.
- Manage your time during the day. Prioritize your work, delegate to others when needed, and remember to take a lunch break. Going outside and enjoying some fresh air or taking a short 10-minute walk will do wonders to keep you refreshed and productive.
- You will be expected to collaborate with others. Never say, "That's not my job" or "That's not my problem." These two statements will ruin your career.
- Resolving a problem is more important than getting credit for taking care of it yourself. Get help when you need it, especially if safety and/ or legality are at stake. A good supervisor will not take it as a sign of weakness if you ask for help when it is genuinely needed.
- In professions dealing with clients or patients, maintain respect and empathy, and keep your professional boundaries. Document the steps you take to resolve a problem, and remember to respect the need for confidentiality.
- Workplaces are divided into departments, offices, or divisions. For work to get done, all parts need to operate collaboratively. Spend time developing relationships with people inside and outside of your department.
- Don't go to your boss with a problem without suggesting a solution. Otherwise you are just complaining. Your boss will think more highly of you if you come in with a solution and will probably be more willing to assist you in the process.

- Admit it when you make mistakes. Maturity is the ability to accept responsibility. You can offset the magnitude of the error by admitting it early and coming up with suggestions to fix it.
- It's acceptable to set boundaries at work. You cannot operate at your best if you are stretched beyond your limits. Delegate responsibilities when prudent. Setting standards for taking on extra projects will make you appear helpful, not hostile.
- Know your limitations but avoid second-guessing yourself. Learn from the past. Take a deep breath, and move ahead.

GETTING ALONG WITH OTHERS

A former supervisor used to say, "People don't have to like one another, but they do have to work together." Nowhere is this statement truer than in the workplace. This is why "getting along with others" is one of the most desired traits by employers. The ability to get along with your office workers or team members will make or break an organization. Dissent with your boss will eventually result in one of you leaving the company (and more often than not, it won't be the boss who will be leaving).

Whenever groups of individuals exist in one space for a period of time, there will be challenges, just like in any relationship. People bring their own baggage, and may react to others with criticism, negativity, gossip, politics, and defensiveness that impedes working relationships. Think about when you had to work together in a group to complete a class or lab project. How well did that usually work out? In my experience there were always one or two people who did all of the work while the others just accepted the credit.

Employees who adopt a people-friendly attitude (empathy for others, willingness to listen nondefensively, a focus on solving problems rather than blaming others, enlisting the help of others, and giving credit to all when they deserve it) will be more successful than those who are not. Customers are keenly receptive to employees' attitudes, and if they're satisfied in how they've been treated, they are more likely to repeat business.

GETTING INVOLVED

Just as studying wasn't the only thing you did when you were in college, there will be other aspects of your day-to-day work as well. Recent grads need to "get involved" in their workplace and participate in committees, company-sponsored community activities, and after-work social activities with coworkers. Even though people are multidimensional beings, we tend to see only one side of an individual at work. Sometimes it's not their best side, either. Interacting with coworkers and workers from other departments in situations outside of work, or their immediate job setting, can show you an entirely different side of an individual. Knowing that John in accounting also plays for a band on the weekends will allow you to view him from a different perspective the next time he questions your budget sheets. And who knows, you may find you have some interests in common and even become friends!

Immersing yourself in company activities can provide you with a sense of belonging, make work more enjoyable, and stretch you personally and professional beyond the confines of your office or lab. Getting involved in activities other than in your immediate work area or responsibilities will give you a glimpse of the "bigger picture" at work and help you be a part of a larger community.

THIRTEEN

Ensuring Marketability in the Future

Life is not about how fast you run or how high you climb but how well you bounce.

—Vivian Komori

The workplace and even the nature of work itself have undergone some major changes in recent years. Unlike in our parents' generation, you will probably not have a job for life. In fact, you should expect to hold a number of jobs in different industries, and be more flexible in the way you actually carry out your work.

Arguably, the largest change agent of the future workplace has been the recent recession. In an article written by the editor of EmploymentDigest.net, the consequence of the recession was that businesses were forced to adapt and restructure the way that they do business. As a result, they learned how to do business on less.

The basic degree will no longer get you a job. In fact, even advanced degrees offer no guarantees. Employers no longer need or want those with basic or general training. Why? Outsourcing. Someone with basic IT skills may be able to keep a company's site up and running, but the company can hire someone overseas for a fraction of the cost. Medical coding specialists, freelance writers, and other computer based professions are in the same boat. And they won't be coming back.[1]

What are job seekers to do? The editor quotes Harvard's mantra that "it is easier to create a job than to find one." His answer: evolve and adapt by taking your skills and developing your own business.

With every new product or upgrade, technology will continue to impact our offices and improve the way we do business. Where you work will not be as tied to a physical location as it was in the past because technology has enabled us to work anywhere. Thanks to video chats over Skype or FaceTime, smart phones, iPads, and laptop computers, you can check in with your boss, send reports to your staff, or hold conference calls with potential clients from any location, at any time of the day or night. Flexibility to work in nontraditional locations may allow workers to better balance work and family obligations, not to mention save time and money on commuting. If you're comfortable with nontraditional modes of work communication, you can prove yourself to be a reliable employee in some companies. This new trend is critical for many professionals who were let go in the recession, because it opened up opportunities for "contractors."

Employee engagement is a big buzzword these days. There have been numerous studies showing that engaged workers—those who buy into the company's mission and values and who are committed to doing a good job at work, not only because they *have* to but because they *want* to. Pitney Bowes defined what engaged employees "look like." In particular, engaged employees "take an active interest in the vision, the productivity and the future growth of the company. They understand how their piece fits in the whole puzzle. They speak well of us [to people outside the company], and they mean it."[2]

The fallout of our recent recession is that layoffs and company closures have wreaked havoc on worker engagement. The consequences of budget cuts and seeing friends and colleagues lose their jobs have created feelings of anxiety and despair in the workers who remained (this was termed the "survivor syndrome" in the early to mid-1990s). During the recession, employers reduced their workforce or did not fill existing positions when employees left or retired. This means that the remaining employees are shouldering additional responsibilities without the added pay or benefits. Those who remain may experience burnout and stress from having to absorb the extra workloads of their departed coworkers—all of which may eventually lead to negativity or pessimism depending on how hard they have been personally impacted by the recession. Trust is hard to rebuild once you've had the "rug pulled from underneath you."

A variety of research studies this year have found that stressed-out, recession-wracked employees are tuning out at work. As a result, employers are once again focusing their attention on employee engagement. Why do employers care how "engaged" their employees are at work? Because worker engagement is tied to their bottom line: sales growth, productivity, and customer loyalty. And good bosses know that to keep employees happy and productive they need to receive the training, emotional support, and resources to cope with the demands of the job. Without those things, employees will become unhappy, negative, or tuned out and will not stay with the company. These are all things that eventually cost the company money.

The Gallup Organization created the Q12, a 12-question survey that identifies strong feelings of employee engagement. Results from the survey show a strong correlation between high scores and superior job performance. In general, the 12 questions deal with topics of having the resources and support needed to do a good job, an employee's connection to the people he or she works with, and an employee's level of commitment to performing quality work.

Today's workers are faced with an environment in which career upheavals occur without warning. Corporate restructuring, downsizing, mergers, and decisions to increase profits affect workers whose jobs were thought to be secure for life. Recent budget problems have even impacted previously thought of "safe" industries such as education, government, and health care.

Salary levels are typically slow to change significantly following a recession, but during the recovery, employers have a willingness to negotiate better deals with current and potential employees. Employers also realize that as the economy improves, employees will gain the confidence to begin to look for other opportunities. This may be a blessing to young graduates entering their career field. Even so, business and industry are generally conservative and there is still a reluctance to hire and to expand the workforce. The other factor to consider is that economic improvement is spotty across the country and does not equally apply across all industries or geographic areas.

THE WORKPLACE OF THE FUTURE

Recently, I registered for a webinar sponsored by Workplace.com, and the introduction of the webinar really caught my attention. Sadly, some of these statements are quite accurate:

The Gold Watch Retirement Party is canceled.

Employment For Life has passed on.

Careerealism site's credo "Because every job is temporary" is being confirmed daily.

Never let your full weight rest on your office chair and keep your personal mementos in a bank box in your car.

We all have images of our grandparents retiring from that one job they worked at for their entire lives. In your parents' generation, the formula for success was simple: graduate from college, get a good job, work hard climbing the ladder of success, and retire in leisure. But now the world has changed. As we begin to recover from our latest recession, many experts are now predicting that the revival will look much different from the recoveries that we've seen in the past; that the future workforce will be made up of a greater number of freelancers and subcontractors.

In a *PBS News Hour* interview, Sudhir Venkatesh, Columbia University professor of sociology, described what he believes the new economic recovery will look like, and that is that we will see a lot of people moving through the labor force for shorter periods of time. "A company may hire someone quickly to fill a job for eight months, a year, a couple of years, and then they're out of work again. . . . The workforce will be characterized by people moving into a company and out of a company instead of the old IBM or Xerox model of the 'company man.' "[3] Venkatesh explains, "Companies can't afford to give someone a job for 10 years and say, we'll hire you for the rest of your life, because they don't know where they're going be in six months or a year. If a company's looking at their future in terms of a very short horizon, then they're going to have to look at their workforce as a flexible workforce."[4]

Today, employability has replaced long-term job security. In the old model of work, the employer provided job security through lifelong employment. Career development and advancement was guaranteed. College graduates today, however, can expect to have seven to eight jobs over their lifetime and will be responsible for their own career development.

Many career experts suggest that you should view your career as a series of temporary job assignments lasting several years at one time. This philosophy implies that one should be continually preparing for their next job as a strategy for future success. Unfortunately, most people are too busy *doing* their jobs to think about where their next job is going to come from. And, let's face it—who really wants to think about finding another job anyway? But in today's world, it may be wise to think about how you can recession-proof your job or, at the least, be able to land on your feet elsewhere if all else fails.

In 2005, a local manufacturing plant in northeastern Pennsylvania closed, laying off 400-plus workers. Many of the unemployed had been with the company for 15–25 years. And many were completely caught unaware when the company closed. They simply did not see the warning signs, despite several years of job consolidations and mini layoffs. They were comfortable in their own world, making a good middle-class salary and enjoying the benefits of seniority with little thought toward the future. When the unthinkable happened and they were laid off, many were not psychologically ready for unemployment. Instead they were surprised and angry. Not only did they have to deal with the emotional aspects of unemployment, but they had to deal with an educational time warp that left them without the technical skills or job-searching strategies needed to apply for another job. Most had no education beyond high school. They had worked at one job, with one skill set all of their lives—learning new skills only when mandated by the company. At 50 years old, many of the employees didn't even know how to use the mouse on their computer, much less apply for a job online!

The employees who had some education beyond high school fared better simply because there were more options open to them. Some found another job, while others went back to school and upgraded their skills or trained for a new profession. I conducted a research study of those employees who enrolled at our college to train for a new career.[5] Although the vast majority found employment after graduation, most earned considerably less than what their salary was when they were laid off. However, most of them enjoyed their work more. One participant commented that her new job was "easier on the body."

All of us need to be more vigilant than ever for how economic changes may affect our careers. Remember that it wasn't too long ago that banking was considered a highly stable career and Wall Street was the place to be for a lucrative and exciting financial career. People in sales, marketing, and research and development are always looking ahead for the next job, customer, or product. These individuals may have an advantage because they always operate in a futuristic mind-set. If you are an introverted individual by nature, or your job requires a great amount of focus, take time at least once a month to come up for air and look around you. Make the effort to talk to people you don't normally interact with (like in the break room or lunchroom), or connect with people via social media, just to see and hear what's going on around you. This approach will pay off in the long run.

Although it's difficult to predict what the future will hold, change is the one constant that we can depend on, so it's probably safe to assume that what people do now in their jobs will be different in the future. Will your new job even exist in its present form 20 years from now? To ensure future viability in the workplace, graduates will need to keep their skills current and their opportunities open.

THE NEW DEFINITION OF CAREER DEVELOPMENT

Today the term *career* goes beyond the boundaries of a single employment setting.[6] The principal features of a career today are:

- Multidirectional rather than linear
- Job mobility across multiple employers
- Personal responsibility for directing one's own career development
- The development of social networks to shape and sustain that career

I like to use the analogy of paddling a canoe down a river to describe the career development process over our lifetime. You can think of the supplies in your canoe as your degree and the skills you acquired, and will acquire, in your first and successive jobs. As you paddle downstream you will encounter obstacles, detours, stops, and starts along your career journey. There are decisions to make along the way. Each new bend in the river may take you in a different direction filled with a new set of situations, opportunities, or obstacles, but each moves you forward.

Several career development professionals, myself included, believe that the focus should be preparing for and finding not a "job"—but a "career." Work should be a lifelong journey that evolves as we grow and experience new things. If you view your job as just a "job," then you are governed by a boss and your opportunities are boxed in by the confines of the organization. Viewing your current job work as just one stepping-stone on a lifelong journey will encourage you to do your best and fuel the desire to learn new material—all the things that employers desire in an employee. Your vision won't necessarily be limited to your current job—it may involve moving on to another company that offers a better environment, more salary, or a chance for promotion, or it may involve going back to school, picking up a new certification, or branching out in a different direction. It is the dynamic not static quality of today's career path that characterizes the new definition of lifelong career development.

CAREER RESILIENCE

Developing "career resilience" is an essential step in the career development process. Resilience is an employee's ability to adapt to adversity in his or her own career development and effectively cope with unexpected changes.[7] Resilience encompasses both strength and flexibility. Resilient people demonstrate flexibility, durability, and an ability to organize and manage ambiguity; are proactive rather than reactive; and have an attitude of optimism and a mind-set that is open to learning. The resilient person is positive and views life as challenging but filled with opportunity. There's no doubt that resilience is emerging as a necessary ability, not only in the context of a person's career and the present economic climate but also as an invaluable tool throughout an individual's life.

Here are some tips on how to develop career resilience:

- Accept that change happens. Embrace rather than resist change.
- Form your identity apart from your job. A job is just one facet of your identity, and a career is just one aspect of your life. To achieve some degree of life balance and resilience, separate who you are from what you do.
- Develop and nurture a broad network of personal and professional relationships. Personal relationships also create a strong base of emotional support.
- Development emotional intelligence. Think creatively and flexibly under stress. Expand rather than shut down when faced with a challenge.
- Focus on the future and gain strength from any new opportunities that may present themselves.
- Practice career self-reliance by benchmarking your skills against standards of excellence in the field and personally committing to an ongoing learning and development plan.

WORK-LIFE BALANCE

No matter how important you think your career is, it is only one part of a balanced life. Most of us have people in our life who we care about and have interests beyond our work. We are spiritual, physical, social, intellectual, creative, and emotional beings. Achieving a healthy balance between our work, family, and personal life involves a delicate balance and nurturing of all aspects of our life.

Work-life balance has evolved out of a relatively recent need to manage stress in our culture. According to Wikipedia, the term *work-life balance* wasn't even used in the United States until 1986, although the term has been around since the mid-1800s.[8] Today, everyone talks about it. If you're an adult student, you know all about juggling the demands of family, work, and school. It creates stress. So do production quotas, added responsibilities due to layoffs, and anxiety over job security. Even the recent advancements in technology that gave us the laptop computer, fax machine, and smart phones do not really make our lives easier, as they were advertised to do. One of the unintended consequences of technology is that being able to multitask just enables us to work *more*. When we begin taking our work home, that's what knocks our work-life balance out of whack. The key to having a healthy work-life balance is a healthy separation between our work and our personal life. We need that separation to recharge and keep ourselves mentally and physically fit so that we *can* contribute 100 percent to our work.

Millennials have watched their parents lose their jobs and retirement benefits after "sacrificing" for a lifetime. The experience of our recent recession has made many workers reevaluate their lives and the role that work plays in their lives. This is why there is a resurgence of values and meaningfulness in work. In the process, Millennials are also redefining what constitutes a fulfilling life. Take some time to ponder the role of work in your life, your personal definition of success, and how you are going to determine when you have reached success.

To prevent overload on the job, take vacations, get away at lunchtime, manage your time effectively, and learn how to diplomatically just say "no." Despite the myth that all of our high-tech technology is supposed to make our lives easier, the reality is that everyone just expects you to be able to accomplish *more* work, not less. There are only eight hours in a day, and only so much work that can be accomplished in a given day. As you are first starting out in your career, you will probably feel the need to overachieve. Granted, it's probably wise to show drive, enthusiasm, and volunteer for new projects. But understand your limitations. You will not impress anyone if you are too emotionally and physically burned-out to be effective in your job. Take care of yourself by getting enough rest, relaxation, time with friends and family, exercise, and good nutrition to combat the effects of stress. And above all else—try to have some fun!

LEAVE ON GOOD TERMS

When you do leave a position (hopefully for a better one), try to leave on good terms. Don't blow up and walk out on the job. We live in such connected times that it's even easier to burn bridges along the way. Always be professional and take the high road. Don't trash your employer on Facebook—you never know who's connected to whom and this may bite you later on when you're interviewing for your next job.

When you decide to leave your position, first inform your immediate supervisor and then tell your colleagues and department staff. Follow up any verbal resignation with a professionally written letter of resignation. Try to be gracious and frame your reasons for leaving in positive terms.

Participate in any exit interviews. Frame your opinions or suggestions for improvement in a helpful manner but don't lie or bad-mouth your boss, your coworkers, or the company.

Give at least two weeks' notice (longer if you are in a management position) and offer to train your replacement. In general, it's probably wise to keep your plans for finding a new job to yourself until you have an actual job offer in hand (I've learned this the hard way). Unless you have an unusually supportive and understanding boss, once you tell him or her you are thinking about leaving, your relationship is never quite the same.

Finish up any projects you were working on, and organize your files so your successor can easily find them. Thank those who supported and mentored you along the way. You want to leave as you entered—like a professional.

CAREER MANAGEMENT

In today's workforce, you are the boss of your own career. This means that you will need to constantly upgrade and learn new things or quickly become obsolete or be replaced (and you thought classes ended with graduation!). Most professions require continuing education and updating of licenses and certifications. In my profession (career counselor), I am required to earn 100 continuing education credits every five years to keep my National Certified Counselor credential. This can be accomplished through a variety of means: attending conferences and webinars, going back to school, or writing publications. For IT professionals, the rate of change is so fast that it becomes a full-time job just to keep up with all of the new products and technologies that come out each year.

Your attitude on the job, in good times and bad, will be key to your career success and to your future employability as you move from one job to another. Strive to become a valuable, hardworking, agreeable employee and you will make yourself valuable to the company and be less likely to be laid off when times get tough. Keep your boss apprised of what you have been doing and what you have accomplished. We will all need to be self-promoters just to make sure others see our value. Career experts state that the art of self-promotion, especially in a supervisory or management position, is one of the main reasons some people are promoted and others are not. They suggest that you should promote yourself by letting your boss know, at the appropriate time, when you have a good idea, have finished an important project, or ran a successful campaign. Women have a tendency to underemphasize their accomplishments, thinking it makes them look like they're bragging, while their male counter-parts feel quite comfortable "tooting their own horn." Speaking up and calmly and factually describing a recent accomplishment is not bragging—it's just reporting what you or your department has been doing. And one final piece of advice—good managers always remember to acknowledge and give credit to those who helped them along the way.

Career management goes beyond landing the first job to focusing on how to be successful in your overall career or in successive jobs over the course of your lifetime. Knowing what you need to do to be successful in your profession, or move up in your organization, is critical to career longevity.

Here are some strategies to ensure career longevity:

1. *Keep your skills updated.* Many of us become so comfortable within our own circle of expertise that we become lax about our professional appearance and lose our connections with the outside world. This actually makes us less secure because we are less aware of changes and, conversely, opportunities, and as a result we become less marketable in the long run. Luckily, most professionals require annual professional development. Many companies sponsor professional development opportunities, so take advantage of them. People in health care or technology careers especially need to remain current in their fields or they will quickly become obsolete. In our ever-changing economy, education is one of the best ways to ensure marketability in your field.

2. *Continue to network.* Stay in contact with professionals in your field, former employers, and former colleagues or clients. These people are an invaluable source of referrals, new ideas, contacts, and information about the future.

3. *Keep a record of your accomplishments*—any professional development activities, training completed, volunteer work, new skills that you have acquired, and the results of projects or assignments. Also, keep copies of performance reviews or evaluations. If your boss is not aware of your contributions, make sure to update him or her about your value to the company.

4. *Ask for feedback.* It's not a bad idea to ask for feedback about your performance at work, especially at the beginning of a new job. Finding a mentor to help you negotiate work politics, or asking for advice in resolving or handling difficult situations are strategies that have been successfully used by many career professionals.

5. *Add value at work*. Be productive and go above and beyond your basic job responsibilities. Volunteer for extra assignments, or volunteer to learn additional job responsibilities or act as a backup for other positions in your department. In the event that positions are slated to be eliminated at your company, you may be seen as someone too valuable to be laid off. Likewise, if you had previously offered to become cross-trained, you may be able to quickly step into another position within your organization if your position is eliminated.

6. *Update your resume once a year*. Use this time to review the past year. Many professionals will routinely do this when submitting an annual report to their boss. Review your personal and professional accomplishments. Ask yourself, what have I accomplished this year? What do I need to accomplish the following year? Are there any skills I need to learn or improve upon? If I lost my job today, would I be able to successfully find another? If not, what would I have to do to become more marketable? Rewrite or update your career summary. Know your market value in your career field. Update your resume, adding any committees that you've served on and/or any publications that you've written, and don't forget community activities. Update the professional organizations you belong to, and the conferences you've recently attended. Reviewing your resume will make you aware of your professional value, should the need to sell your skills arise.

7. *Be aware of current events*. Stay abreast of market, industry, and technological trends that may affect your career field. Current social, political, and economic events affect some industries more than others. This is where talking to outside professionals may help by providing you with valuable outsider information. Being able to spot future trends not only will give you time to prepare for a position shift in the event of a corporate merger, layoff, or change in company mission but will ensure that you will not be caught off-guard.

8. *Keep an eye open for possibilities*. Why? Because when you do need them, you'll have all of the resources you need to make the transition. Some people routinely scan job openings (and some even apply for these jobs) just to keep up on what's out there in the marketplace. Opportunities present themselves to people who are open to receiving them. New ideas for products, new ventures, and new partnerships are happening all around you; if don't get outside of your office or lab, or talk to people outside of your department

or company, you'll never be aware of them. This is where joining professional organizations or the "groups" feature on LinkedIn comes in handy: it helps you stay current with the newest ideas, issues, and events happening in your profession.

As you develop self-confidence, skills, and experience you will find it easier to broaden your range of options, thus enabling you to move into higher levels of responsibility or into job opportunities where you can make better use of your skills and abilities. None of your education or work experience is ever wasted. I still occasionally use things I learned in my former (and now totally unrelated) undergraduate degree that I never thought I would ever use again.

The career management process doesn't stop once you get your first job; it continues throughout your lifetime. As we move through life, we will (hopefully) continue to upgrade our careers in terms of better pay and advancement, less stress, better working conditions, fewer hours, and more job security. I wish you continued happiness and success in your career.

APPENDIX A

Sample Resumes, Cover Letters, and LinkedIn Summaries

SAMPLE EXERCISE SCIENCE RESUME

Jill M. Daniels
44 First Street   Phone: (570) 991-7412
Wilkes-Barre, Pennsylvania   E-mail: Jill4@yahoo.com

QUALIFICATIONS SUMMARY
- Knowledge in the areas of exercise, health, and wellness
- Exceptional interpersonal and customer service skills
- Works well independently and as a team member

EDUCATION

East Stroudsburg University, Stroudsburg, PA, expected graduation May 2012

Bachelor of Science, Exercise Science/Fitness Leadership, GPA 3.6/4.0

Minor: Business Management

HONORS

Kappa Omicron Nu Honor Society

President's List, 4 semesters

COURSE HIGHLIGHTS

Exercise Physiology: Analyzed the structure, function, and exercise training responses of numerous physical fitness tests.

Nutrition and Wellness: Identified and interpreted caloric output through a three-day computer diet program analysis.

Planning and Organization of Physical Education: Actively participated in a class community project for a Cancer Awareness Walk/5 K Run through fund-raising, event day setup/breakdown, and registration.

CERTIFICATIONS

American Red Cross, CPR/AED certified, August 2011

MEMBERSHIPS

American College of Sports Medicine, 2010–Present

Health Awareness Club

WORK EXPERIENCE

Waitress

Timbers at Mohegan Sun at the Pocono Downs, Plains, PA, 2008–Present

Commended for commitment to providing quality service.

SAMPLE COMPUTER INFORMATION SCIENCES RESUME

JOHN SMITH
4545 North Main Street, Nanticoke, PA 18634
570.740.1234
jsmith@spix.net

SUMMARY

Accomplished Computer Information Technology student with a solid background in client-side web design. Creative self-starter eager to begin a career with a progressive company that utilizes innovative technology.

EDUCATION

Luzerne County Community College, Nanticoke, PA
• **A.A.S., Computer Information Systems:** expected graduation May 2012

- 3.8 GPA
- Dean's List, Fall and Spring 2011

AREAS OF KNOWLEDGE

LANGUAGES: C++, RPG IV, Visual Basic.NET, JAVA
OPERATING SYSTEMS: OS/400, Windows XP, 7
SOFTWARE: Adobe Dreamweaver, Microsoft Word 2010,
Microsoft Access 2010, Microsoft Excel 2010, Microsoft
PowerPoint 2010

EXPERIENCE

2010–Present   Mr. Z's Food Markets, Inc., Mountaintop, PA
Baker/Stock Clerk
- Bake donuts, decorate cakes, and prepare breads.
- Stock shelves and prepare inventory reports.

Summers 2008–2010   PG Energy, Wilkes-Barre, PA
Lawn Care Assistant
- Maintained company grounds (cut grass, trimmed bushes, and painted fencing).
- Organized lawn care equipment room.

ORGANIZATIONS

- CIS (Computer Information Systems) Club, Vice President, 2011
- CIS (Computer Information Systems) Club, Member, 2010–Present

SAMPLE TRADITIONAL COVER LETTER

Sally Smith
49 North Street
Wilkes-Barre, PA 18701

November 1, 2012

Thomas Jones
ABC Supply Company
49 Market Street
Hazleton, PA 18620

Dear Mr. Jones:

Thank you for discussing opportunities at your company at the recent job fair at Trinity University. I am very interested in the photography position at your company.

I am accustomed to working in an environment where customer service and people skills are a priority. My strengths include a passion for photography and the ability to organize and prioritize assignments. In short, I enjoy taking pictures and being around people. At our recent annual student photography exhibit, I won first place in both the Color Composition and Black-and-White Still categories.

I have attached my resume and portfolio for your review. Please feel free to call me to arrange a convenient day and time to discuss the position further. Thank you in advance for your time and consideration, and I look forward to meeting with you.

Sincerely,
(Signature)
Sally Smith

SAMPLE E-LETTER

To: tjones@supply.aol
Subject: Photography Position
Dear Mr. Jones,

Thank you for discussing opportunities at your company at the recent job fair at Trinity University. I am very interested in the photography position that became available at your company.

From my previous customer service positions, I am accustomed to working in an environment where customer service and people skills are a priority. My strengths include a passion for photography and the ability to organize and prioritize assignments. In short, I enjoy taking pictures and being around people. At our recent annual student photography exhibit, I won first place in both the Color Composition and Black-and-White Still categories.

I have attached my resume and portfolio for your review. Please feel free to call me at 570.740.1234 to discuss the position further. Thank you for your time and consideration, and I look forward to meeting with you.

Sincerely,
Sally Smith
(Place ATTACHMENT here)

SAMPLE LINKEDIN SUMMARIES

Accomplished computer information technology graduate with a solid background in client-side web design. Creative and eager self-starter who recently designed websites for three local nonprofit organizations.

Recent graduate looking for work as a data specialist in the greater New York City area. BA in business administration with concentrations in economics and international studies.
Specialties: Microsoft Office, research, data.

I am an electrical engineering graduate with prior retail management experience. I financed my education by working part-time while maintaining full-time status and a 4.0 GPA. I am looking for an entry-level position in electrical engineering.

APPENDIX B

Sample Job Titles and Potential Employers

(An advanced degree is required for those occupations marked with an *.)

AGRICULTURE

Sample Job Titles

Agribusiness manager

Environmental scientist

Animal scientist

Biosystems engineer

Construction manager

Crop and soil scientist

Entomologist

Environmental economist

Fisheries and wildlife

Food industry manager

Food scientist

Forester

Horticulturist

Landscape architect

Dairy farmer/rancher

Potential Employers

Family/corporate dairy farms
Colleges/universities
State/federal government
Food manufacturing companies
Genetics corporations
Farm equipment manufacturers
Wood products companies
Grass/turf seed companies
Seed companies
Horticulture companies
Farm bureau
Chemical companies

ART

Sample Job Titles

Billboard artist/sign painter
Gallery owner/operator
Artist-in-residence
Museum publications director
Cartoonist
Web-page designer
Art teacher
Arts fundraiser
Book/CD cover designer
Art director
Art librarian*
Arts council director
Illustrator
Picture framer
Art therapist*
Community arts center director
Greeting card artist

Art appraiser

Museum education coordinator

Conservator/restorer*

Medical illustrator

Visual merchandiser

Grants specialist

Museum curator

Police/courtroom artist

Audiovisual specialist

Historical preservation coordinator*

Photographer

Art auctioneer

Art critic/reporter

Exhibit designer

Scenic artist (film/theater)

Corporate art consultant

Mural artist

Arts and humanities council director

Printmaker

Arts lawyer*

Graphic designer

Potential Employers

Advertising agencies

Colleges/universities

Sign shops

Art galleries

libraries

Art supply stores

Public relations firms

Magazines/newspapers

Printing firms

Online/mail-order companies

Publishing companies

Museums
Textile industry
Amusement parks
Retail stores
Schools
TV/film industry
Greeting card companies
Auction houses
Recreation departments
Corporate communication departments
Photo agencies
Camps
Restoration firms
Media production companies
Lawyers

MUSIC
Sample Job Titles
Musician
Composer
Recording engineer
Sound mixer
Music educator
Music director
Music/video producer
Music critic

Potential Employers
Television/radio/film
State/federal government
Churches
Colleges/universities
Elementary/secondary schools
Private studios

Private/community music schools
Production companies
Theaters
Performance organizations
Libraries
Record companies
Cruise lines
Magazines and newspapers

PHOTOGRAPHY

Sample Job Titles

Portrait photographer
Studio photographer
Freelance photographer
Photojournalist

Potential Employers

Portrait studios
Retail centers
Colleges/universities
Newspapers/magazines
Television stations
Companies (online products)

THEATER

Sample Job Titles

Actor/actress
Company manager
Theater teacher*
Development director
Artist-in-residence
Director/producer
Box office manager

Arts fund-raiser

Scenic designer

Theater librarian*

Lighting designer

Business manager*

Drama therapist*

Voice-over artist

Personal manager

Audience relations specialist

Coordinator hair/makeup

Artist's agent

Community arts center director*

Costume designer

Booking agent

Managing director*

Special effects technician

Acting coach

Stage manager

Literary agent*

Public relations director

Dramaturg

Potential Employers

Community organizations

Educational/cultural institutions

Fundraising firms

Television/radio/film

Production companies

Colleges/universities/schools

Theatres

Touring companies

Arts councils

Performing arts organizations

Libraries

Amusement and theme parks
Cruise lines
Film companies
Entertainment law firms

AUTOMOTIVE
Sample Job Titles
A+ diagnostic technician
Aftermarket automotive sales rep
Air conditioning specialist
Automotive store manager
Manufacturers representative
Automotive master technician
Automotive parts salesperson
Automotive technician
Automotive service attendant
Lead brake specialist
Electronic system diagnostic specialist
Emission control specialist
Insurance adjustor
Service manager
Service writer
Warranty clerk
Chassis and body designer/fabricator
Motorsports electronics technician
Racing team pit crew
High-performance service technician

Potential Employers
Auto parts distribution center
Automotive repair facility
New/used-car dealerships
Car insurance company

Racing teams
Department of motor vehicles
Retail/wholesale companies
High-performance parts manufacturer
Engine research and development companies
Aftermarket sales or manufacturing companies

BUSINESS

Accounting

Sample Job Titles

Accountant
Junior accountant
Accounting clerk
Accounts payable/receivable
Bookkeeper
Business analyst
Certified Public Accountant
Corporate accountant
Auditor
Collection manager
Financial representative
Underwriter
Loan officer administrator
Internal Revenue Service investigator
Bank officer
Comptroller

Potential Employers

Accounting firms
Business offices in private companies
Manufacturing plants
Educational institutions
Hospitals
Government

Insurance companies

Banks and credit unions

Financial services

Actuary

Sample Job Titles

Actuary

Actuarial scientist

Risk manager

Auditor

Budget analyst

Benefits administrator

Financial analyst

Investment banker

Government statistician

Risk and insurance specialist

Securities analyst

Trust analyst

Potential Employers

Accounting firms

Insurance companies

Research facilities

Pension fund companies

Health care industry

Private corporations

Financial institutions

Government agencies

Investment firms

Business consulting companies

Business Management

Sample Job Titles

Account executive

Account manager

Benefits manager

Credit manager

Consultant

Corporate trainer

Recruiter

Executive director

Inventory manager

Business manager

Sales representative

Small-business owner

Training specialist

Wage and salary administrator

Retail manager

Distribution manager

Administrator

Bank president

Hotel manager

Human resource manager

Nursing home administrator

Public administrator

Urban planner

Stadium manager

Potential Employers

Private corporations

Banks

Hospitals

Public schools/colleges/universities

Retail stores

Management consultants

Manufacturing plants

Local/city/state government

Nonprofit agencies
Human services agencies
Accounting firms
Finance offices
Insurance companies
Social services organizations
Self-employment
Utility companies

COMMUNICATIONS
Advertising
Sample Job Titles
Copywriter
Editor
Art/creative director
Public relations
Graphic designer
Promotions director
Marketing director
Social media manager
Account executive
Product development
Marketing research manager

Possible Employers
Private corporations/businesses
Advertising agencies
Marketing companies
Print shops
Promotional companies
Banks/credit unions
Hospitals
Colleges/universities

Radio/Television Broadcasting

Sample Job Titles

DJ

Program director

New/traffic reporter

Station manager

Promotions assistant

Camera operator

News anchor

Master control operator

News reporter

Production assistant

Sports show talk host

Play-by-play announcer

Sports producer

Stadium announcer

Sports editor

Voice-over talent

Video editors

Field technician

Potential Employers

Radio stations

Television stations

Film production companies

Internet radio stations

Video production companies

Digital/cable television networks

Communications

Sample Job Titles

Fund-raiser

Advertising manager

Public relations

Press agent
Public information officer
Communications specialist
Social media manager
Copywriter
Account executive
Creative director
Sales manager
Media buyer
Development officer
Volunteer coordinator
Publicity manager

Potential Employers
Nonprofit organizations
Private corporations
Educational institutions
Hospitals
Advertising agencies
Television/radio stations
Government administration
Newspapers/magazines
Media production companies

Journalism
Sample Job Titles
Reporter
Editor
Author
Copywriter
Script writer
Publisher
Speech writer
Insurance underwriter

News service researcher

Technical writer

Social media manager

Acquisitions editor

Librarian*

English teacher

Proofreader

Public relations specialist

Publications researcher

Screen writer

Potential Employers

Radio/television companies

Newspaper/magazines

Private corporations

Nonprofit organizations

Colleges/universities

Advertising/marketing companies

Book publishers

Insurance companies

Private businesses

Manufacturing companies

COMPUTER SCIENCE/INFORMATION TECHNOLOGY

Sample Job Titles

Help-desk technician

Computer animator

Computer support specialist

Applications analyst

Business analyst

Database programmer

Computer programmer

PC support specialist

Network administrator

Operations research specialist

Software developer

Systems manager

Technical sales representative

Cyber security specialist

Technical support

Technical writer

User support specialists

Field service technician

Potential Employers

Graphic design companies

Video game design companies

Retail companies

Internet companies

Schools and universities

Advertising/marketing departments

Consulting firms

Businesses

Manufacturing companies

Local/state/federal government

Banks

Financial institutions

Central Intelligence Agency (CIA)

Health care facilities

Law enforcement agencies

Corporate security offices

Federal Bureau of Investigation (FBI)

Private security consultants

Research laboratories

Retail stores

U.S. Department of Justice

Engineering firms

Computer services companies

Software manufacturers

Internet providers

Data processing companies

Telecommunications companies

Utility companies

Airlines

Casinos

CRIMINAL JUSTICE

Sample Job Titles

Local/state police officer

FBI/Secret Service

Security guard

Loss prevention specialist

Probation officer

Juvenile detention specialist

Drug enforcement agent

Criminologist/forensic scientist

Correctional officer

Attorney*

Judge*

Court clerk

Homeland Security agent

Border Patrol officer

Private detective

Forensic psychologist*

Adjudicator*

Airline security specialist

Arson investigator

Bailiff

Child welfare caseworker

Crime laboratory analyst

Criminal investigator

Customs agent/inspector

FBI/Secret Service agent

Hotel security director

Law clerk

Parole officer

Polygraph examiner

Private investigator

Victim advocate

Potential Employers

County/state/federal government

U.S. court system

Private corporations

Airports

Private security firms

State crime laboratories

Private detection agencies

Correctional institutions

Colleges/universities

Hospitals

Correctional institutions

Local/state police departments

Banks

FBI/CIA/Secret Service

Community transition programs

Corporate security offices

Crisis centers

Diplomatic services/embassies

Drug Enforcement Agency

Federal Trade Commission

Government agencies

U.S. Citizenship and Immigration Services

Juvenile justice

Law firms

Probation departments
Research industries
Retail stores
U.S. Customs
U.S. Department of Justice
U.S. Postal Inspection Service

FORENSIC SCIENCE

Sample Job Titles

Criminologist
Crime scene investigator
Forensic pathologist*
Forensic scientist
Forensic entomologist
Forensic anthropologist*
Forensic psychiatrist*
Forensic science technician

Potential Employers

County/state crime labs
Police departments
Private medical/DNA/paternity drug labs
FBI/Drug Enforcement Agency/Bureau of Alcohol, Tobacco, Firearms and Explosives
Armed forces
Secret Service
U.S. Postal Service
Research labs

EDUCATION

Sample Job Titles

Early childhood/elementary teacher
Middle school teacher

High school teacher

College professor*

Tutor

ESL teacher

Reading specialist*

School counselor*

School psychologist*

Educational sales

Educational trainer

Educational editor/writer

Grant administrator

Environmental educator

Potential Employers

Public/private/cyber/charter schools

College/universities

Day care centers

Private learning centers

Human services agencies

Churches/religious organizations

Private educational companies

Educational book/magazine publishers

National park system

ENGINEERING

Sample Job Titles

Aerospace engineer

Biomedical engineer

Civil engineer

Chemical engineer

Design engineer

Industrial engineer

Mechanical engineer

Electrical engineer

Surveying engineer

Associate engineer

Project engineer

Structural engineer

Test engineer

Applications engineer

Plant engineer

Process engineer

Environmental engineer

Nuclear engineer

Quality control engineer

Software engineer

Traffic engineer

Robotics engineer

Potential Employers

City/county/state/federal government

Power industry

Engineering firms

Utility companies

Engineering consulting firms

General contractor

Licensed surveyor

Petrochemical industry

U.S. military

Defense industry

Communications industry

Aerospace industry

Manufacturing industry

Consumer products industry

Colleges/universities

HEALTH CARE

Dental Assisting/Hygiene

Sample Job Titles

Dental assistant

Expanded functions dental assistant

Dental hygienist

Dental products salesperson

Dental office manager

Dental instructor*

Potential Employers

Private dental offices

Periodontal/oral surgery clinics

Dental laboratories

Dental equipment companies

Armed forces

Correctional institutions

Nursing

Sample Job Titles

Medical/surgical nurse

ER nurse

Hospice nurse

Nurse educator*

Pediatric nurse

School nurse

Geriatric nurse

Nurse anesthetist*

Intensive care nurse

Legal nurse consultant*

Office nurse

Maternal infant nurse

Neonatal nurse

Nurse practitioner

Nurse supervisor (head nurse)

Surgical nurse

Occupational health nurse

Oncology nurse

Psychiatric nurse

Public health nurse

Rehabilitation nurse

Researcher*

Teacher/instructor*

Potential Employers

Private physician offices

Hospitals

Outpatient clinics

Personal care facilities

Correctional institutions

Hospice centers

Public schools/colleges/universities

Armed services

Peace Corps

Medical centers

Birthing centers

Summer/day camps

Biotechnical companies

Cancer treatment centers

Community health clinics

Emergency medical centers

Home health companies

Rehabilitation centers

Industry/business

Insurance companies/HMOs

Mental health centers

Migrant centers

Private homes

Public health departments

Research centers

HEALTH EDUCATION

Athletic Trainer/Exercise Science

Sample Job Titles

Athletic trainer

Coach

Team physician*

Kinesiologist

Exercise physiologist

Physical therapist*

Sporting goods sales

Sports/recreation camp director

Athletic director*

Physical fitness instructor

Fitness consultant

Physical trainer

Golf pro

Strength and conditioning coach

Sport physical therapist*

Sport administrator

Resort manager

Sports official

Potential Employers

Health and fitness centers

YMCA/YWCA

Professional sports teams

Sports medicine clinics

Health care facilities

Private corporations
Sporting goods stores
Professional Golf Association/Ladies Professional Golf Association
Golf courses
Camps
College/universities
Community recreational facility
Clubs/resorts
Olympic centers

Nutrition/Dietetics

Sample Job Titles

Clinical dietician
Nutritionist
Clinical nutrition manager
Director, child nutrition program
Food service manager
Pharmaceutical sales representative
Health educator*
Gerontological nutritionist
Lactation consultant
Sports nutritionist
Health consultant
Research dietician

Potential Employers

Hospitals/health care facilities
Personal care homes
Social services agencies
Athletic teams
4-H/cooperative extension
Colleges/universities
Private corporations
Pharmaceutical companies

HOSPITALITY

Culinary

Sample Job Titles

Chef

Cook

Sous chef

Quality control technician

Banquet manager

Caterer

Food Critic

Teacher/professor*

Potential Employers

Restaurants

Hotels

Catering companies

Cruise lines

Resorts

Food manufacturers

Bakeries

Grocery stores

Schools

Hospitals

Colleges/universities

Hotel and Restaurant Management

Sample Job Titles

Assistant manager

Banquet manager

Caterer

Conference coordinator

Convention services director

Food and beverage manager

Food broker

Operations manager

Owner/operator

Sales director

Purchasing director

Property managers

Facility managers

Executive housekeeper

Hotel manager

Meeting/conference coordinator

Banquet and catering manager

Convention services manager

Food and beverage director

Restaurant manager

Director of sales and marketing

Tour operators

Potential Employers

Restaurants

Hotels/motels

Corporations

Resorts

Cruise lines

Casinos

Theaters

Stadiums

Schools/colleges/universities

Hospitals

Taverns

Fast-food operators

Travel agencies

Spas

Bed and breakfast operations

Catering companies

Cruise ships

Convention halls
Visitors bureaus

LIBERAL ARTS
English
Sample Job Titles
Copy editor
Columnist
Freelance writer
Editor
Fact checker
Proofreader
Promotions manager
Social media manager
Reporter
Researcher
Librarian*
Author
Script writer
Poet
Teacher/professor*
News director
Anchor
Television/radio producer
Public relations assistant
Account executive
Press secretary
Speech writer
Technical writer
Fund-raiser

Potential Employers
Radio/television stations
Communications companies

Advertising/marketing agencies
Book/magazine publishers
Newspapers
Online media companies
Private corporations
Government agencies
Schools/colleges/universities
Public relations firms

History
Sample Job Titles
Anthropologist
FBI/CIA agent
Archeologist*
Foreign news correspondent
Lawyer*
Archivist
Biographer
Genealogist
Librarian*
Community relations director
Historian
Historic preservationist*
Historic site your guide
Historical society staff
Museum curator
History teacher/professor*
Writer
Documentary editor/producer

Potential Employers
Museums and archives
Schools/colleges/universities
Travel and tourism services

Broadcasting corporations
Libraries
Historical societies
Publishers
National Geographic
Bureau of the Census
State/federal government
Foundations
Nonprofit organizations
National park system

Political Science
Sample Job Titles

Legal assistant/paralegal
Lawyer*
Judge*
Government official
Lobbyist
Congressional aide
Pollster
Political consultant
Legislative correspondent
Chief of staff
Campaign manager
Assessor
Market research/analyst
Labor relations specialist
Demographer
Insurance agent
Intelligence analyst
Peace Corps/Vista worker
Editor
International relations

Political scientist
Policy analyst
Professor*
Press secretary
Urban administrator
Economic developer
Public relations specialist
Victim advocate
Nonprofit executive
Fund-raiser

Potential Employers

Business and industry
CIA
U.S. State Department
Peace Corps/Vista
Public interest groups
Research foundations
Legislators
Social and welfare services
State and local governments
FBI
Housing and community development
Political parties

Psychology/Counseling/Human Services

Sample Job Titles

Counselor*
Human services aide
Social worker*
Licensed psychologist*
School counselor*
Career counselor*

Rehabilitation counselor*

Vocational/employment counselor*

Addictions counselor

Marriage and family counselor*

Music/art therapist*

Animal-assisted therapist*

Industrial psychologist

Forensic psychologist*

Psychometrician

Psychology teacher/professor*

College counselor/psychologist*

College academic advisor*

(Bachelor's-level psychology majors can also find entry-level positions in business and government.)

Potential Employers

Human services agencies

Community counseling agencies

Private clinics

Hospitals

Local/state/federal government

Rehabilitation clinics

Private corporations

Public/private schools

Colleges/universities

Private practice

Correctional institutions

State/county hospitals

RECREATION, PARKS, AND TOURISM MANAGEMENT

Sample Job Titles

Golf course manager

Camp leader

Environmental educator/interpreter
Park ranger
Scout leader
Guide

Potential Employers

Parks/nature centers
Historic sites
Camps
Private outfitters/adventure
Local/state/federal parks
Commercial outdoor facilities
Municipal/state/federal government
Recreation divisions of the armed services
YMCA/YWCA
United Way agencies
Scouting organizations
University student unions
Alumni services
Nonprofit organizations
Golf industry

SCIENCE

Sample Job Titles

Astronomer
Biologist
Biochemist
Biotechnologist
Chemist
Forensic scientist
Researcher
Environmental scientist
Dentist*

Optometrist*
Soil scientist
Geneticist
Horticulturist
Meteorologist
Physicist*
Zoologist*
Technical writer
Researcher
Editor
Physician*
Chiropractor*
Pharmacist*
Veterinarian*
Laboratory technologist
Quality assurance

Potential Employers

Schools/colleges/universities
Research centers
Government agencies
U.S. Department of Agriculture
Military
Pharmaceutical companies
Chemical companies
Oil/gas companies
Genetics companies
NASA
Book/magazine publishers
Hospitals/health care facilities
Television studios
Private practice
Manufacturing plants
Food production companies

BIOLOGY

Sample Job Titles

Biologist

Biological researcher

Biochemist

Botanist

Ecologist

Fish and game warden

Plant pathologist

Pharmaceutical sales representative

Teacher/professor*

Science editor/writer

Potential Employers

Food research facilities

Pharmaceutical companies

Genetics companies

Colleges/universities

Magazine and book publishers

MATHEMATICS

Sample Job Titles

Computer programmer*

Researcher*

Statistician

Actuary

Consultant

Teacher/professor*

Financial analyst

Economist

Actuary

Mathematician

Computer/software designer*

Market researcher

Mathematical modeler/tester

Technical writer

Potential Employers

Computer industry

Research firms

Insurance companies

Schools/colleges/universities

Testing services

Finance industry

Brokerage firms

Government

Banks

Accounting firms

APPENDIX C

Sample Interview Questions (by Major)

GENERAL INTERVIEWING ADVICE

About.com (http://jobsearch.about.com/cs/interviews/a/aceinterview.htm)

Job Interview Questions (http://www.jobinterviewquestions.org)

Monster (http://career-advice.monster.com/job-interview/interview-questions/100-potential-interview-questions/article.aspx)

The Riley Guide (http://www.rileyguide.com/interview.html)

QuintCareers (http://www.quintcareers.com)

SAMPLE MAJOR-SPECIFIC INTERVIEW QUESTIONS

Art

1. Tell us something about the art projects you have worked in your previous jobs.
2. Give me an example of your creativity.
3. What is your favorite medium and why?

Business

Accounting

1. What accounting courses did you like best? Least? Why?
2. Which accounting applications do you know?

3. Explain the advantages as well as disadvantages of different accounting systems.

4. Being able to learn quickly on the job is important. Tell me about a situation when you had to pick up an essential skill quickly.

Business Management

1. Name some SDLC methodologies.

2. If you had to take corrective measures to address continuous poor performance by an employee, what would they be?

3. We are interested in how you show initiative to go beyond everyday requirements.

4. Give me an example of when you showed initiative at school or at work.

5. What is your management philosophy?

6. Where do you see yourself in five years?

7. What was the last book you read?

Finance

1. Describe what you believe to be the future of the derivatives market.

2. What is 0.125 squared?

3. How would you go about selling the idea of a derivatives hedge to a prospective client?

4. Two retail banks have different return rates on their loan portfolios, although default rates are similar. What might explain the difference?

5. How can you convince your client that the "higher yield" bond does not really give a higher yield?

6. How would you go about valuing a firm? How would you value a hotel in Chicago if you had only one day to look around?

7. Give some suggestions to improve the credit card business of your bank.

8. What is the relationship between the forward and spot interest rate?

9. What is the difference between enterprise value multiples and P/E multiples?

10. How does depreciation affect the three financial statements?

11. About what price was the Dow Jones today?

12. Would you rather have a dollar today or two dollars tomorrow?

Marketing

1. What is the difference between marketing and sales?
2. Why do you think you are suitable for this job?
3. What are the advantages/disadvantages of the cold-calling process in telemarketing?
4. Tell me your plans and strategy as a marketing officer.
5. Sell me this pen.
6. If you were to introduce a new product into a foreign market, what are some of the factors you would first study in that country?
7. Tell me something that is not on your resume.
8. What experience have you had with sales and cold calls?
9. Discuss your experience with public speaking.
10. How would you bring in new clients to our business?

Sales

1. What do you see as the key skills in closing a sale?
2. What do you dislike about sales?
3. How do you feel about making cold calls?
4. How do you move on from a rejection?

Pharmaceutical Sales

1. Tell me why you are interested in pharmaceutical sales.
2. Why do you want to work at (name of company)?
3. Tell me what you know about (company) and where you found the information.
4. Tell me about an accomplishment that you are most proud of.
5. Are you competitive? How?
6. Describe a difficult challenge in your professional life and how you overcame it.

Communications

Advertising

1. Why do you want to pursue a career in advertising?
2. Give me some examples of your innovation.

Journalism/Writing/Editing

1. When did you start writing?
2. How are your grammar and punctuation?
3. What experience have you had interviewing people?

Criminal Justice

Forensic Science

1. What interested you in pursuing a career in forensic science?
2. What skills do you believe are essential in this career? Do you think you have those?
3. Do you think your knowledge about forensic science is strong enough to implement it on crime investigation?
4. How do you handle stress and adverse situations?

Health Care

Dental Assisting/Hygiene

1. Do you have any chairside experience?
2. What made you decide to become a dental assistant?
3. Do you have any laboratory experience (casts of teeth, temporary crowns, etc.)?
4. Do you have any office experience?
5. Are you CPR certified?
6. What does teamwork mean to you?
7. Why are you interested in joining our office?
8. What procedure do you use for sterilizing and disinfecting dental equipment in order to prepare for surgery?
9. Show me how you would organize the applicable instruments for each procedure.

Education

1. How confident are you about teaching students for whom English is not their first language?
2. What methods do you use to evaluate your success as an instructor?
3. How comfortable are you with a diverse classroom?

4. How do you handle unruly students who actively disrupt the classroom?

5. Are there any methods of instruction you plan to implement to make teaching more interesting for the students?

6. How do you handle a child who seems gifted but is a discipline problem?

7. What would you expect your students to have gained after having you as a teacher?

8. How would you handle a parent who disagrees with your grading method or an assignment?

9. What does it mean to be a teacher?

10. What part of teaching do you look forward to most? The least?

11. (See http://roadtoteaching.com/teacher-interview-questions for more interview questions.)

Special Education

1. Students are going to be at different stages of development. How do you address the needs of those who require extra instruction while still progressing the rest of the students through the syllabus?

2. What personality traits do you feel make you qualified for dealing with children with developmental disabilities?

3. Are there any types of behavioral disorders you feel you would be unequipped to handle?

4. What disabilities, disorders, and handicaps have you had experience instructing and in which do you believe you could use extra instruction?

5. Do you believe students with mental or developmental disabilities should be enrolled in regular education classes if they have the potential to succeed?[1]

Engineering

1. Tell me about the most challenging engineering project that you have been involved with during past year.

2. Describe a time when you confronted a problem that really tested your engineering know-how.

3. What is your overall career objective? Do you see yourself working in engineering 10 years from now?

4. Give me an example of a time when you applied your ability to use analytical techniques to define problems or design solutions.

5. Tell me about a time when a project team effort that you were involved in failed.

6. How can you best use your engineering education and prior work experience to help our company grow?

7. What single technical skill or ability is your best asset?

Health Care

Nursing

1. Why did you choose nursing as your career?
2. What is your favorite type of patient?
3. Describe a situation where you feel you really helped a patient.
4. Describe your least favorite patient and situation.
5. How do you handle stress?
6. Why would you make a good nurse on this floor?
7. What was your favorite clinical experience?
8. What is one thing that you have done as a student nurse that changed the course of treatment for a patient?
9. How do you handle problems with coworkers?
10. How do you handle criticism?
11. Have you ever made a mistake or found a mistake that someone else made and what did you do about it?
12. Where do you see yourself in 10 years?

Personal Training

1. Why did you choose a career in personal fitness training?
2. Are you certified in CPR and first aid?
3. How do you motivate people?

Hospitality Management

1. How do you handle negative feedback from a very angry customer? How do you respond to him or her?
2. How do you envision good hotel management?
3. What are your career goals?

4. If you needed to organize a party or meeting for some customers, how would you do it?

5. How do you interact with staff? How do you motivate them?

6. What do you know about our business? What do you think about our services/staff?

7. What do you think makes us different in the market?

8. What do you think are main characteristics a hospitality manager should always possess?

9. How have you responded in the past when your replacement calls in sick and a substitute will take over an hour to come in?

10. Give an example of when you did something without being asked. Can you give me another example?

11. Tell me about your most frustrating experience as a (job title).

12. Why do you think dependability is important for a restaurant cook?

13. As a cook, if you see an increase or decrease in customer flow, how do you respond?

14. If you see product getting low, what would you do?

15. How would you handle not having everything in stock that you need to make the item you are assigned?

16. The restaurant is busy, and you are tired, short-handed, and have not had a day off in six days. How does this affect your work and attitude?

17. How do you handle complaints about meals you have prepared?

18. What steps would you take to ensure your job is done in your allotted amount of time?

19. Tell me about a time you saw a coworker taking out food they did not pay for.

20. Your boss changes the special. What would you do?

Information Technology

1. What programs are you familiar with?

2. Write a function that deletes every other element in a linked list.

3. Think about a project you recently worked on. What were some design decisions, design trade-offs, or implementation choices that had to be made on the project?

Help Desk

1. A user says that he is not able to get online when he attempts to connects to the Internet on an XP computer system. Explain what you should do.

2. If the monitor shows a blank blue screen after restarting your computer, what would be the best way to resolve this major problem?

Science

Microbiology/Medical Laboratory

1. Describe your field experience including sample type collected, sampling techniques, field measurements taken, and equipment used.

2. Describe your experience with analytical chemistry. Do you have experience with organic extractions and/or sediment or tissue digestions?

3. Do you know what trace metal clean technique is? Please describe.

4. Please describe your experience with and/or knowledge of quality assurance and quality control analysis.

5. Describe your experience with analytical instrumentation.

6. What is your experience with word processing, text editing, e-mail, and data management with the use of spreadsheets and databases. What programs have you used?

7. Describe a time when you had to meet strict deadlines. What percentage of those deadlines were you able to meet? What were the contributing factors in them not being met?

8. What do you consider when organizing your work?

9. Describe a past situation in which you worked as a member of a team. What was your role in the team?

10. This job requires working with radioisotopes and carcinogens. Please describe your experience working with these, and the methods used for safe handling. Does working with these present any difficulties for you?

11. Give an example or two of the types of repetitive tasks you have had to perform, how often you performed them, and how you ensured a high level of accuracy while doing repetitive tasks.

12. Describe the level of supervision you have received in the past and the type of work you did independently.

General Science

1. What do you know about our company?
2. Tell us about the last research project you worked on.
3. How good are your practical laboratory skills?
4. How would you go about solving a scientific problem?
5. Give an example of when you had to communicate effectively.
6. Describe how you work in a team.
7. What specialized equipment would you need for _____?

Biology

1. What are examples of homeostasis?
2. How does caffeine affect plant growth?
3. How do leaves change color?

Chemistry

1. How would you separate naphthalene and benzoic acid?
2. What is the purpose of a 2.4 DNP test?
3. Is water an element or a compound?

Genetics

1. Is genetic engineering the best solution?
2. What is heterozygote detection?
3. What ethical dilemmas should be considered when genetic engineering is put into practice?

APPENDIX D

Job Search-Related Websites

GENERAL JOB SEARCH WEBSITES

All County Jobs (http://www.allcountyjobs.com)

CareerBuilder (http://www.careerbuilder.com)

Indeed (http://www.indeed.com)

JibberJobber (http://www.jibberjobber.com)

Job Hunt (http://www.job-hunt.org)

Juju (http://www.job-search-engine.com)

LinkUp (http://www.linkup.com)

Monster (http://www.monster.com)

SimplyHired (http://www.SimplyHired.com)

INDUSTRY-SPECIFIC EMPLOYMENT SITES

Accounting

Accounting Jobs Today (http://www.accountingjobstoday.com)

American Institute of CPAs (http://www.aicpa.org)

Art

ARTSEARCH (http://jobs.artsearch.us)

Automotive

AUTOjobs.com (http://www.autojobs.com)

Business

Careers-in-Business (http://www.careers-in-business.com)

Computer Science/IT

Dice (http://www.dice.com)

Construction

Construction Jobs (http://www.constructionjobs.com/index_eng.cfm)

Chemistry

American Chemical Association (http://chemistryjobs.acs.org/jobs)

Court Reporters/Broadcast Captioning

National Court Reporters Association (http://www.ncra.org)

National Verbatim Reporters Association (http://www.nvra.org)

Criminal Justice

Police Employment (http://www.policeemployment.com)

U.S. Department of Justice (http://www.justice.gov/careers/careers
.html)

Officer.com (http://www.officer.com)

911 Hot Jobs (http://www.911hotjobs.com)

Culinary

American Culinary Federation (http://www.acfchefs.org)

Hcareers (http://www.hcareers.com)

Hotel Jobs (http://www.hoteljobs.com)

Dental Assisting and Hygiene

Dental Assistant Jobs (http://www.dentalassistantjobshelp.com)

Dentalworkers.com (http://www.dentalworkers.com)

DentalPost.net (http://www.dentalpost.net)

Education

Teachers-Teachers.com (http://www.teachers-teachers.com)

Chronicle of Higher Education (http://chronicle.com/section/Home/5)

Engineering

Engineer.net (http://www.engineer.net)

Graduating Engineer (http://www.graduatingengineer.com)

(Search for jobs on engineering professional organization websites such as the American Society of Civil Engineers.)

Entertainment

EntertainmentCareers.Net (http://www.entertainmentcareers.net)

Federal Jobs

USA Jobs (http://www.usajobs.gov)

Forensics

American Academy of Forensic Sciences (http://www.aafs.org)

Crime Scene Investigator Network (http://www.crime-scene-investigator .net/index.html)

Finance

eFinancial Careers (http://www.efinancialcareers.com)

Finbox (http://www.finbox.com)

Green Jobs

Green Careers Guide (http://www.greencareersguide.com)

SustainLane (http://www.sustainlane.com/green-jobs)

Health Careers

ADVANCE (http://health-care-jobs.advanceweb.com)

AllHealthcareJobs.com (http://www.allhealthcarejobs.com)

MedicalWorkers.com (http://www.medicalworkers.com)

Therapy Jobs Zone (http://www.therapyjobszone.com)

Hospitality

Hcareers (http://www.hcareers.com)

Hoteljobs.com (http://www.hoteljobs.com)

Travel-hospitality-jobs.com (http://www.travel-hospitality-jobs.com)

Human Resources

Society for Human Resource Management (http://www.shrm.org/jobs)

Journalism

JournalismJobs.com (http://www.JournalismJobs.com)

Nonprofit

Idealist (http://www.idealist.org)

Opportunity Knocks (http://www.opportunityknocks.org)

Psychology, Counseling, Human Services

American Psychological Association (http://www.apa.org)

American Counseling Association (http://www.counseling.org)

Association for Psychological Science (http://www.psychological
science.org)

Publishing

Book Jobs (http://bookjobs.com)

Physics

Physics & Astronomy Online (http://www.physlink.com)

Purchasing and Supply Management

Institute for Supply Management (http://www.ism.ws)

Retail

AllRetailJobs.com (http://www.allretailjobs.com)

Theatre

BackstageJobs.com (http://backstagejobs.com)

Urban Planning

American Planning Association (http://www.planning.org)

Individuals with Disabilities

GettingHired (http://www.GettingHired.com)

SimplyHired (http://www.SimplyHired.com)

RESEARCH COMPANIES

Business.com (http://www.business.com)

CorporateInformation.com (http://www.corporateinformation.com)

Glassdoor (http://www.Glassdoor.com)

National Center for Charitable Statistics (http://nccsdataweb.urban.org/
PubApps/search.php)

ReferenceUSA (http://www.ReferenceUSA.com)

Vault (http://www.Vault.com)

Yahoo Ticker Symbol Lookup (http://finance.yahoo.com/lookup)

SALARY INFORMATION

JobStar (http://www.JobStar.org)

PayScale (http://www.Payscale.com)

Salary.com (http://www.Salary.com)

Notes

INTRODUCTION

1. McKinsey and Company, "An Economy That Works: Job Creation and America's Future," McKinsey Global Institute, June 2011, http://www.mckinsey.com/mgi/publications/us_jobs/pdfs/MGI_us_jobs_full_report.pdf (accessed September 13, 2011).

2. National Center for Education Statistics, "Degrees Conferred by Degree-Granting Institutions, by Level of Degree and Sex of Student," 2011, http://nces.ed.gov/programs/digest/d10/tables/dt10_279.asp?referrer =report (accessed October 26, 2011).

CHAPTER 1

1. T. Denham, "Career Development Myths of College Students," Timesunion.com, blog entry, September 9, 2011, at 5:00 A.M., http://blog.timesunion.com/careers (accessed September 10, 2011).

2. Bureau of Labor Statistics, "Job Openings and Labor Turnover Survey Highlights," December 2011, http://www.bls.gov/web/jolts/jlt_labstatgraphs.pdf (accessed February 26, 2012).

3. National Association of Colleges and Employers, "Class of 2011 Took Longer to Land Jobs," August 17, 2011, http://www.naceweb.org/s08172011/job_search_time (accessed September 25, 2011).

4. Smeal College of Business, "Internships/Co-ops," http://ugstudents.smeal.psu.edu/careers/internships-co-ops (accessed September 27, 2011).

5. National Association of Colleges and Employers, *Job Outlook 2011* (Bethlehem, PA: National Association of Colleges and Employers, November 2010).

6. S. Freeman, "Winning the Face-to-Face Interview by 'Leading the Witness'—Do You WANT to Do the Job," CareerCenterToolbox.com, 2011, http://www.careercentertoolbox.com/interviews/winning-the-face -to-face-interview-by-leading-the-witness (accessed August 3, 2011).

7. A. Farnham, "Background Checks Now Include Twitter, Facebook," ABC News, June 24, 2011, http://abcnews.go.com/Business/job -tweets-background-checks-employers-now-include-postings/story?id =13908874 (accessed October 24, 2011).

CHAPTER 2

1. L. Pollak, "Getting Started on LinkedIn: Advice for Recent Grads," Louisianajobnetwork.com, May 23, 2011, http://www.louisianajob network.com/articles/title/Getting-Started-on-LinkedIn-Advice-for-Recent -Grads/5420/315 (accessed October 24, 2011).

CHAPTER 3

1. National Association of Colleges and Employers, "What Matters in a Resume?" press release, November 18, 2011, http://www.naceweb.org/ Press/Releases/What_Matters_in_a_Resume_.aspx (accessed November 18, 2011).

CHAPTER 4

1. V. Bostwick and R. Angulo, *2011 Entry-Level Job Search Report: Insights on Recruiting the Next Generation of Talent* (San Francisco: AfterCollege, 2011).

2. C. Russell, "How to Spot a Good Job Board," Recruitingblogs.com, blog, August 16, 2011 at 9:10 A.M., http://www.recruitingblogs.com/ profiles/blogs/how-to-spot-a-good-job-board (accessed August 17, 2011).

3. J. Dickler, "The Hidden Job Market," CNNmoney.com, http:// money.cnn.com/2009/06/09/news/economy/hidden_jobs (accessed August 2, 2011).

4. Bostwick and Angulo, *2011 Entry-Level Job Search Report.*

5. J. Light, "For Job Seekers, Company Sites Beat Online Job Boards, Social Media," *Wall Street Journal*, April 4, 2011, http://online.wsj.com/ article/SB10001424052748703806304576236731318345282.html

?KEYWORDS=job+search+company+websites (accessed August 14, 2011).

6. National Association of Colleges and Employers, "Social Media in the Job Search: LinkedIn, Twitter Outpace Facebook as Tools," June 8, 2011, http://www.naceweb.org/s06082011/social_media_job_search (accessed August 19, 2011).

7. Ibid.

8. R. Shindell, "Branding Yourself to be 'Headhunted,' Part 1," CareerCenterToolboxcom, 2011, http://www.careercentertoolbox.com/personal-strategy/branding-yourself-to-be-headhunted-part-1 (accessed June 25, 2011).

9. P. Weddle, "How Recruiters Work and Why," CareerCenterToolboxcom, 2011, http://www.careercentertoolbox.com/personal-strategy/how-recruiters-work-and-why (accessed June 28, 2011).

10. Selloutyoursoul.com, "The Ultimate Guide to Finding a Job as an English Major," May 27, 2011, http://www.selloutyoursoul.com/2011/05/27/the-ultimate-guide-to-finding-jobs-as-an-english-major (accessed October 24, 2011).

11. Ibid.

12. M. A. Wasmuth, "Find Your Nonprofit Job," Wordpress.com, blog, August 15, 2011, http://mawinfo.wordpress.com/2010/09/04/finding-your-nonprofit-job (accessed August19, 2011).

CHAPTER 5

1. G. Chrispin and M. Mehler, *10th Annual CareerXroads Source of Hire Report: By the Numbers*, CareerXroads, March 2011, http://www.careerxroads.com/news/SourcesOfHire11.pdf (accessed October 24, 2011).

2. Jobvite, *Jobvite Social Recruiting Survey 2011*, 2011, http://web.jobvite.com/rs/jobvite/images/Jobvite-SRP-2011.pdf (accessed September 3, 2011).

3. Society for Human Resource Management, *SHRM Poll: Social Networking Websites for Identifying and Staffing Potential Job Candidates*, June 20, 2011, http://www.shrm.org/Research/SurveyFindings/Articles/Pages/SocialNetworkingWebsitesforIdentifyingandStaffingPotentialJob Candidates.aspx (accessed November 11, 2011).

4. R. Haefner, "More Employers Screening Candidates via Social Networking Sites," CareerBuilder.com, June 10, 2009, http://www.careerbuilder.com/Article/CB-1337-Interview-Tips-More-Employers-Screening-Candidates-via-Social-Networking-Sites (accessed October 24, 2011).

5. WilliamarrudaReach.com, "Personal Branding Guru, William Arruda," YouTube video, Reach Personal Branding, May 5, 2009, http://www.youtube.com/watch?v=6paItEm2AF4 (accessed October 24, 2011).

6. J. Light, "Recruiters Rethink Online Playbook," *Wall Street Journal*, January 18, 2011, http://online.wsj.com/article/SB100014240 52748704307404576080492613858846.html (accessed August 15, 2011).

7. L. Margolin, "21 Mistakes People Make on LinkedIn," Lion Club Job Search.com, August 8, 2011, http://www.lioncubjobsearch.com/2011/08/21-mistakes-people-make-on-linkedin.html (accessed August 24, 2011).

8. Society for Human Resource Management, *SHRM Poll*.

9. National Association of Colleges and Employers, "Social Media in the Job Search: LinkedIn, Twitter Outpace Facebook as Tools," June 8, 2011, http://www.naceweb.org/s06082011/social_media_job_search (accessed August 19, 2011).

10. Society for Human Resource Management, "SHRM Poll."

CHAPTER 6

1. Fine Arts Career Services, "A Career Guide for Studio Art Majors," University of Texas at Austin, May 2008, http://www.utexas.edu/finearts/sites/default/files/attach_download/career_guide_for_studio_art_majors.pdf (accessed September 15, 2011).

2. R. Bernstein, "Highlights from a National Survey of U.S. Employers," news release, May 17, 2011, http://newsfeed.academyart.edu/wp-content/uploads/2011/05/poll-summary.pdf (accessed July 8, 2011).

3. G. Howard, "How Do I Get a Job in the Record Industry?" artistshouseMUSIC.org, November, 4, 2006, http://www.artistshouse music.org/articles/how+do+i+get+a+job+in+the+record+industry? (accessed October 7, 2011).

4. J. Goldberg, *Great Jobs for Music Majors* (New York: VGM Career Books, 2005).

5. Accounting Education Change Commission, *Objectives of Education for Accountants*, Position Statement No. One (Sarasota, FL: AECC, September 1990).

6. K. A. McIntosh, "Portfolio Tips for an Accounting Clerk Job Interview," eHow.com, February 3, 2011, http://www.ehow.com/info_7891012_portfolio-accounting-clerk-job-interview.html#ixzz1Z5bhA79C (accessed November 11, 2011).

7. Careers-in-Accounting.com, "Accounting: Skills and Talents," http://www.careers-in-accounting.com/acskill.htm (accessed November 12, 2011).

8. College of Arts and Sciences, "Resumes," Ohio State University, https://asccareerservices.osu.edu/files/asccareerservices/Actuarial %20Science%20Resume.pdf (accessed October 14, 2011).

9. CollegeGrad.com, "Degree Programs for Advertising Marketing PR: Online and Campus Schools," 2011, http://www.collegegrad.com/ careers/manag03.shtml (accessed October 18, 2011).

10. EverydayInterviewTips.com, "Marketing Job Interview Questions and Answers," http://www.everydayinterviewtips.com/questions-and -answers/marketing-job-interviews#ixzz1Z5Vddvx0 (accessed November 11, 2011).

11. K. Sundheim, "4 Ways to Dramatically Improve Your Sales Inter-viewing," kasplacement, September 26, 2011, http://kensundheim.com/ 2011/09/26/4-ways-to-dramatically-improve-your-sales-interviewing (accessed November 13, 2011).

12. WetFeet.com, "Broadcasting," http://www.wetfeet.com/careers -industries/careers/broadcasting (accessed October 18, 2011).

13. T. Rogers, "What Can 2011 Journalism School Graduates Expect in the Job Market?" About.com, http://journalism.about.com/od/ careersinjournalism/a/What-Can-Journalism-School-Graduates-Expect -In-The-Job-Market.htm (accessed November 11, 2011).

14. D. Rohn, "Newspaper Clips: How Many Should You Include in Your Application?" JournalismJobs.com, http://www.journalismjobs. com/career_advice.cfm#4 (accessed October 17, 2011).

15. S. Nuri, "The Requirements to Become a Criminal Justice Profes-sional," eHow.com, http://www.ehow.com/info_7926423_requirements -become-criminal-justice-professional.html#ixzz1cBhq6VSS (accessed October 29, 2011).

16. T. Roufa, "Getting Ahead in Your Criminology Career: Learn How to Better Your Chances for Promotion," About.com, http:// criminologycareers.about.com/od/Career_Advancement/a/Getting-Ahead -In-Your-Criminology-Career.htm (accessed October 29, 2011).

17. AllCriminalJusticeSchools.com, "A Forensic Scientist Answers the Question: 'What Is Forensic Science?'" http://www.allcriminal justiceschools.com/legal-careers/forensics/forensic-scientist-career-interview (accessed October 24, 2011).

18. E. Lions, "What Are Engineering Employers Looking For?" IEEE.org, May 2006, http://www.todaysengineer.org/2006/may/jobhunt .asp (accessed November 11, 2011).

19. Sloan Career Cornerstone Center, "Mechanical Engineering Over-view," http://www.careercornerstone.org/pdf/me/mecheng.pdf (accessed November 11, 2011).

20. M. Rurak, "Employers Are Looking to Hire Multifaceted Chemical Engineers," Jasneek.com, http://www.jasneek.com/jobseekers/employers_are_looking_to_hiremul.asp (accessed October 24, 2011).

21. Hcareers.com, "Breaking into Hospitality: Tips and Hints for Non-traditional Jobseekers," http://www.hcareers.com/us/resourcecenter/tabid/306/articleid/214/default.aspx (accessed October 24, 2011).

22. Hcareers.com, "Crystal-Ball Gazing: Top Trends in the Hospitality Industry," http://www.hcareers.com/us/resourcecenter/tabid/306/articleid/278/default.aspx (accessed October 24, 2011).

23. L. Estrada, "The Hiring Process at Apple, Sample Questions and Insight from Real Applicants," Edible Apple, September 13, 2011, http://www.edibleapple.com/the-hiring-process-at-apple-sample-questions-and-insight-from-real-applicants (accessed September 15, 2011).

24. J. Spolsky, "Advice for Computer Science College Students," Joelonsoftware.com, January 2, 2005, http://www.joelonsoftware.com/articles/CollegeAdvice.html (accessed August 17, 2011).

25. Ibid.

26. D. Gehlhaus, "What Can I Do with My Liberal Arts Degree?" *Occupational Outlook Quarterly* 51, no. 4 (Winter 2007–2008):5.

27. VancouverAquariumMarineScienceCenter.org, "AquaFacts: Career as a Marine Biologist," http://www.vanaqua.org/education/aquafacts/marinebiologist.html (accessed October 24, 2011).

CHAPTER 7

1. L. J. Townsel, "Working Women: Dressing for Success," *Ebony* 51, no. 11 (1996): 60–65.

2. Polk-Lepson Research Group, "2010 Professionalism in the Workplace, York College of Pennsylvania, August 2010, http://www.ycp.edu/media/yorkwebsite/cpe/York-College-Professionalism-in-the-Workplace-Poll—2010.pdf (accessed August 1, 2011).

3. Ibid.

4. Ibid.

5. Ibid.

6. Ibid.

7. K. B. LaSala and J. Nelson, "What Contributes to Professionalism?" *MEDSURG Nursing* 14, no. 1 (2005): 63–67.

8. Ibid.

9. Ibid.

10. Ibid.

11. R. Half, "Graduate Gaffes," news release, The Creative Group, May 3, 2011, http://creativegroup.mediaroom.com/techetiquette (accessed July 8, 2011).

12. G. W. Waldner, "The 5 Secrets to Getting a Job after Graduation," Fox News, May 13, 2011, http://www.foxnews.com/opinion/2011/05/13/5-secrets -getting-job-graduation/#ixzz1TnakmWwJ (accessed November 12, 2011).

CHAPTER 8

1. L. Pollack, "10 Tips for Using Social Media in Your Job Search," *Job Choices 2012 Diversity Edition* (Bethlehem, PA: National Association of Colleges and Employers, 2011).

2. E. Tahmincioglu, "Employers Turn to Tests to Weed Out Job Seekers," msnbc.com, August 15, 2011, http://today.msnbc.msn.com/id/ 44120975/ns/business-personal_finance (accessed November 12, 2011).

3. A. Shadday, "Assessments 101: An Introduction to Candidate Testing," Workforce Management Online, January 2010, http://www .workforce.com/archive/feature/recruiting-staffing/assessments-101 -introduction-candidate-testing/index.php (accessed September 1, 2011).

4. D. Dugan, "Body Talk: What Your Body Language Says about You," Salary.com, http://www.salary.com/Articles/ArticleDetail.asp ?part=par4348 (accessed September 1, 2011).

5. Ibid.

6. Lundquist College of Business, "The Career Step Series Step 4: Interviewing," University of Oregon, http://www2.lcb.uoregon.edu/App_Themes/ Content/Docs/Career/Interviewing.pdf (accessed November 14, 2011).

CHAPTER 9

1. L. Ryan, "Eight Job-Interview Wins for the Record Book," BusinessWeek.com, May 27, 2011, http://www.businessweek.com/managing/ content/may2011/ca20110526_722311.htm (accessed August 19, 2011).

2. JobInterviewQuestions.org, "Illegal Interview Questions," 2011, http://www.jobinterviewquestions.org/questions/illegal-questions.asp (accessed October 27, 2011).

CHAPTER 10

1. A. Wrzesniewski, C. McCauley, P. Rozin, and B. Schwartz, "Jobs, Careers, and Callings: People's Relations to Their Work," *Journal of Research in Personality* 31, no. 1 (1997): 21–33.

2. I. D. Yalom, *Existential Psychotherapy* (New York: Basic Books, 1980).

3. F. Herzberg, B. Mausner, and B. B. Snyderman, *The Motivation to Work*, 2nd ed. (New York: Wiley, 1959).

4. E. M. Morin, H. E. C. Montréal, and C. Gagné, "Making Work Meaningful," http://www.irsst.qc.ca/media/documents/PubIRSST/R-644 .pdf (accessed September 10, 2011).

5. M. G. Pratt and B. E. Ashforth, "Fostering Meaningfulness in Working and at Work." In K. Cameron, J. Dutton, and R. Quinn (Eds.), *Positive Organizational Scholarship: Foundations of a New Discipline* (San Francisco: Berrett-Kohler, 2003).

6. D. Pink, *Drive: The Surprising Truth about What Motivates Us* (New York: Riverhead Books, 2009).

7. Ibid.

8. Ibid.

9. NYPost.com, "Poll: Most in US Don't Like Their Jobs," January 5, 2010, http://www.nypost.com/p/news/business/poll_most_in_us_don _like_their_jobs_4iRFvxrVqLk3mxtMVmCULO#ixzz1YQChvlPD (accessed September 19, 2011).

10. Gaebler.com, "Employee Engagement Statistics," http://www .gaebler.com/Employee-Engagement-Statistics.htm (accessed September 1, 2011).

11. American Psychological Association, "Stress in America," press release, 2010, http://www.apa.org/news/press/releases/stress/key -findings.aspx (accessed November 10, 2011).

12. M. Smith, R. Segal, and J. Segal, "Understanding Stress Symptoms, Causes, and Effects," Helpguide.org, October 2011, http://helpguide.org/mental/stress_signs.htm (accessed November 10, 2011).

13. V. Bostwick and R. Angulo, *2011 Entry-Level Job Search Report: Insights on Recruiting the Next Generation of Talent* (San Francisco: AfterCollege, 2011).

CHAPTER 11

1. M. E. Ghilani, "Applying the Concept of Mental Toughness to the Job Search Process," National Career Development Association, May 2011, http://associationdatabase.com/aws/NCDA/pt/sd/news _article/43065/_PARENT/layout_details_cc/false (accessed September 25, 2011).

2. R. Shindell, "Job Hunting in an Economic Downturn." *careercentertoolbox.com* (2011), http://www.careercentertoolbox.com/the-career-planning-process/jobs-hunting-in-an-economic-downturn (accessed September 15, 2011).

CHAPTER 12

1. M. Horton, "The Generation Gap in Your Office," Socialcast.com, blog, http://blog.socialcast.com/the-generation-gap-in-your-office-2 (accessed October 24, 2011).
2. E. Short, "Thoughts on the 40-Hour Workweek from a Gen Y'er," Comerecommended.com, blog, July 15, 2011, http://comerecommended.com/blog/2011/07/15/thoughts-on-the-40-hour-workweek-from-a-gen-yer (accessed September 10, 2011).
3. University of Tennessee Career Services, "Success after Graduation," http://career.utk.edu/resources.php (accessed September 26, 2011).
4. N. Barry, *When Reality Hits: What Employers Want Recent College Graduates to Know* (Dallas, TX: Brown Books, 2007).
5. CareerBuilder.com, "College Hiring 2005," news release, http://www.careerbuilder.com/share/aboutus/pressreleasesdetail.aspx?id=pr169&sd=4%2F13%2F2005&ed=12%2F31%2F2005 (accessed November 3, 2011).
6. Michigan State University Career Services, "12 Essentials for Success: Competencies Employers Seek in College Graduates," http://careernetwork.msu.edu/pdf/Competencies.pdf (accessed November 3, 2011).

CHAPTER 13

1. Editor, "How the New Economy Has Changed the Job Market," EmploymentDigest.net, http://employmentdigest.net/2011/09/how-the-new-economy-has-changed-the-job-market (accessed October 24, 2011).
2. G. Kranz, "Special Report on Employee Engagement: Losing Lifeblood," *Workforce Management*, July 2011, http://www.workforce.com/archive/feature/hr-management/special-report-employee-engagement-losing-lifeblood/index.php (accessed October 24, 2011).
3. PBS.org, "Sudhir Venkatesh on the New Meaning of Recovery," http://www.pbs.org/newshour/businessdesk/2009/08/sudhir-venkatesh-on-the-new-me.html (accessed October 24, 2011).
4. Ibid.

5. M. E. Ghilani, "Displaced Workers Successfully Reenter the Workforce: Postgraduation from a Community College," *Community College Journal of Research and Practice* 32, no. 8 (2008): 573–81.

6. R. J. DeFilippi and M. B. Arthur, "The Boundaryless Career: A Competency-Based Perspective," *Journal of Organizational Behavior* 15 (1996): 307–24.

7. R. H. Waterman Jr., J. D. Waterman, and B. A. Collard, "Toward a Career-Resilient Workforce," *Harvard Business Review*, July 1994, http://hbr.org/1994/07/toward-a-career-resilient-workforce/ar/1 (accessed November 10, 2011).

8. Wikipedia, "Work-Life Balance," http://en.wikipedia.org/wiki/Work%E2%80%93life_balance (accessed November 20, 2011).

APPENDIX C

1. Everyday Interview Tips, "Teaching Interview Questions and Answers," http://www.everydayinterviewtips.com/questions-and-answers/teaching-job-interviews (accessed November 30, 2011).

Index

About the Author

Mary E. Ghilani, M.S., NCC, is the Director of Career Services at Luzerne County Community College in Pennsylvania. She is a National Certified Counselor and has been working with college students for over 18 years. She is the author of three books: *Second Chance: How Career Changers Can Find a Great Job, 10 Strategies for Reentering the Workforce, Web-Based Career Counseling,* and numerous career-related articles.

Edwards Brothers Malloy
Thorofare, NJ USA
August 6, 2012